MACAT

An Analysis o₁

Franz Boas's

Race, Language and Culture

Anna Seiferle-Valencia

Published by Macat International Ltd
24:13 Coda Centre, 189 Munster Road, London SW6 6AW.

Distributed exclusively by Routledge
2 Park Square, Milton Park, Abingdon, Oxon OX14 4RN
711 Third Avenue, New York, NY 10017, USA

Routledge is an imprint of the Taylor & Francis Group, an informa business

www.macat.com
info@macat.com

Cataloguing in Publication Data
A catalogue record for this book is available from the British Library.
Library of Congress Cataloguing-in-Publication Data is available upon request.
Cover illustration: Capucine Deslouis

ISBN 978-1-912302-01-7 (hardback)
ISBN 978-1-912128-38-9 (paperback)
ISBN 978-1-912128-26-6 (e-book)

Notice

CONTENTS

THE MACAT LIBRARY

The Macat Library is a series of unique academic explorations of seminal works in the humanities and social sciences – books and papers that have had a significant and widely recognised impact on their disciplines. It has been created to serve as much more than just a summary of what lies between the covers of a great book. It illuminates and explores the influences on, ideas of, and impact of that book. Our goal is to offer a learning resource that encourages critical thinking and fosters a better, deeper understanding of important ideas.

Each publication is divided into three Sections: Influences, Ideas, and Impact. Each Section has four Modules. These explore every important facet of the work, and the responses to it.

This Section-Module structure makes a Macat Library book easy to use, but it has another important feature. Because each Macat book is written to the same format, it is possible (and encouraged!) to cross-reference multiple Macat books along the same lines of inquiry or research. This allows the reader to open up interesting interdisciplinary pathways.

To further aid your reading, lists of glossary terms and people mentioned are included at the end of this book (these are indicated by an asterisk [*] throughout) – as well as a list of works cited.

Macat has worked with the University of Cambridge to identify the elements of critical thinking and understand the ways in which six different skills combine to enable effective thinking.
Three allow us to fully understand a problem; three more give us the tools to solve it. Together, these six skills make up the **PACIER** model of critical thinking. They are:

ANALYSIS – understanding how an argument is built
EVALUATION – exploring the strengths and weaknesses of an argument
INTERPRETATION – understanding issues of meaning

CREATIVE THINKING – coming up with new ideas and fresh connections
PROBLEM-SOLVING – producing strong solutions
REASONING – creating strong arguments

To find out more, visit **WWW.MACAT.COM.**

CRITICAL THINKING AND *RACE, LANGUAGE AND CULTURE*

Primary critical thinking skill: INTERPRETATION
Secondary critical thinking skill: CREATIVE THINKING

Franz Boas's 1940 *Race, Language and Culture* is a monumentally important text in the history of its discipline, collecting the articles and essays that helped make Boas known as the 'father of American anthropology.'

An encapsulation of a career dedicated to fighting against the false theories of so-called 'scientific racism' that abounded in the first half of the 20th-century, *Race, Language and Culture* is one of the most historically significant texts in its field – and central to its arguments and impact are Boas's formidable interpretative skills. It could be said, indeed, that *Race, Language and Culture* is all about the centrality of interpretation in questioning our assumptions about the world.

In critical thinking, interpretation is the ability to clarify and posit definitions for the terms and ideas that make up an argument. Boas's work demonstrates the importance of another vital element: context. For Boas, who argued passionately for 'cultural relativism,' it was vital to interpret individual cultures by their own standards and context – not by ours. Only through comparing and contrasting the two can we reach, he suggested, a better understanding of humankind.

Though our own questions might be smaller, it is always worth considering the crucial element Boas brought to interpretation: how does context change definition?

ABOUT THE AUTHOR OF THE ORIGINAL WORK

Born in Germany in 1858, to Jewish parents, **Franz Boas**'s work challenged the pseudoscientific support of racism, including anti-Semitism. He first received a doctorate in physics from the University of Kiel, but after doing some fieldwork changed his focus to anthropology. Boas founded the first PhD program in anthropology on American soil, at Columbia University, and established a distinctly American style in the discipline. A prolific writer, he died in New York City in 1942 at the age of 84.

ABOUT THE AUTHOR OF THE ANALYSIS

Dr Anna Seiferle-Valencia holds a doctorate in anthropology from the University of Harvard.

ABOUT MACAT

GREAT WORKS FOR CRITICAL THINKING

Macat is focused on making the ideas of the world's great thinkers accessible and comprehensible to everybody, everywhere, in ways that promote the development of enhanced critical thinking skills.

It works with leading academics from the world's top universities to produce new analyses that focus on the ideas and the impact of the most influential works ever written across a wide variety of academic disciplines. Each of the works that sit at the heart of its growing library is an enduring example of great thinking. But by setting them in context – and looking at the influences that shaped their authors, as well as the responses they provoked – Macat encourages readers to look at these classics and game-changers with fresh eyes. Readers learn to think, engage and challenge their ideas, rather than simply accepting them.

'Macat offers an amazing first-of-its-kind tool for
interdisciplinary learning and research. Its focus on works
that transformed their disciplines and its rigorous approach,
drawing on the world's leading experts and educational institutions,
opens up a world-class education to anyone.'

Andreas Schleicher
**Director for Education and Skills, Organisation for Economic
Co-operation and Development**

'Macat is taking on some of the major challenges in university
education ... They have drawn together a strong team of active
academics who are producing teaching materials that are
novel in the breadth of their approach.'

Prof Lord Broers,
former Vice-Chancellor of the University of Cambridge

'The Macat vision is exceptionally exciting. It focuses
upon new modes of learning which analyse and explain seminal texts
which have profoundly influenced world thinking and so social and
economic development. It promotes the kind of critical thinking
which is essential for any society and economy.
This is the learning of the future.'

Rt Hon Charles Clarke, former UK Secretary of State for Education

'The Macat analyses provide immediate access to the critical
conversation surrounding the books that have shaped their
respective discipline, which will make them an invaluable resource
to all of those, students and teachers, working in the field.'

Professor William Tronzo, University of California at San Diego

WAYS IN TO THE TEXT

KEY POINTS

- Franz Boas was a key figure in the founding of American and modern anthropology. Born in 1858 in Germany, he died in 1942 in New York City.

- *Race, Language and Culture* argues that all human cultures have value and that we must consider each in its own historical context. The work also debunks theories of scientific racism* (the use of pseudoscientific methods, theories, and hypotheses to support racist categorizations of human beings).

- This text marks a watershed in the development of American anthropology, establishing the scope, aims, and methods of the discipline; its theoretical contributions continue to be relevant to scholarship today.

Who Was Franz Boas?

Franz Uri Boas, the author of *Race, Language and Culture* (1940), was born in 1858 in Minden, a town in the German region of Westphalia. The son of educated, non-practicing Jews, Boas became interested in the fields of natural history and geography* at an early age. This interest persisted for his entire life. He studied physics, mathematics, and geography at various universities and graduated from the University of Kiel* (a seat of learning in northern Germany) in 1881 with a doctorate in physics. After graduation, Boas went on a geographical research project to Baffin Island* in Canada, a place populated by the indigenous—native—Americans known as Inuit;* there he began to develop his understanding of anthropology. He would go on to become a founding figure in the development of the field, even referred to as the "father of American anthropology."

Boas's work changed theory and practice both in fieldwork*—studies of people conducted in the places where they live—and in classrooms, laboratories, and museums. He also made a lasting impact on the discipline through his work as a museum curator, author, and professor. In addition to publishing six books and over 700 articles, he taught and mentored many of the great thinkers in the field.

Boas is also notable for the significant contributions he made though a lifelong commitment to social and racial justice. He was an outspoken critic of scientific racism, eugenics* (the movement to "improve" human genetics through selective breeding and sterilization), and social and political racism. He attacked the racist policies of the Nazi* party—the extreme right-wing governing party of Germany during World War II*—as early as 1933. During World War II, the Allied forces* led by the US and Britain smuggled his anti-Nazi pamphlets into Germany. Although he was a secular* (non-practicing) Jew, Boas experienced discrimination due to both his Jewish heritage and his status as an immigrant. Professionally and personally, he was committed to using anthropology to challenge contemporary ideas of social and scientific racism. He died in New York City in 1942.

What Does *Race, Language and Culture* Say?

In many ways, the overarching message of *Race, Language and Culture* is respect for individual cultures. The text emphasizes that human diversity is best explained by culture. Boas saw every culture as unique, valuable, and best understood through the lens of its own history.

As a scholar, Boas was clearly ahead of his time. Other scholars of his era argued that moral and mental characteristics could be connected to certain physical types, or races, and that some races were superior to others. But throughout his career, Boas insisted on the value of all cultures. He advocated social justice for communities of color, especially the African American community. In *Race, Language and Culture*, Boas uses anthropology to prove that each culture has equal value. This message remains as relevant today as it was in 1940 when this work first appeared.

The book itself is a collection of articles Boas wrote on various topics. Some sections present the results of research projects, while others make more general statements about broader topics. The chapters offer an overview of the scholarship of Franz Boas throughout a half-century of his career. The chapters also show how Boas applied his theories to the practice of anthropology. For Boas, theory and practice influence one another. Scholars of anthropology still discuss the relationship between theory and practice today.

Some 75 years after its initial publication, *Race, Language and Culture* still speaks to the field of anthropology. It is a foundational text in the study of anthropology and the history of the discipline. Almost all anthropology programs require students to read Boas—and the most frequently assigned articles can be found in the pages of *Race, Language and Culture*.

The theoretical contributions Boas made in this text also remain useful to today's scholars, although in some cases his research methods are now outdated. Anthropological methods were still developing during Boas's time. They continued changing after the publication of this book in 1940 and continue to do so today. But however dated some of his methodology, the main ideas Boas presents in this work continue to be relevant.

Race, Language and Culture is also useful for understanding the work of later scholars. During his years as a professor, Boas trained many students who went on to become leaders in the field. These include the US anthropologists Ruth Benedict,* Margaret Mead,* Edward Sapir,* and Alfred Kroeber* as well as the novelist Zora Neale Hurston,* who trained as an anthropologist. Each of these scholars also made significant contributions to the field of anthropology as teachers and scholars. Reading Boas deepens our understanding of their work.

Why Does *Race, Language and Culture* Matter?

Race, Language and Culture is undoubtedly a key text in the history of American anthropology. Boas originated key ideas in anthropology, such as cultural relativism* (the idea that the behavior, beliefs, and actions of an individual are best understood in the context of that person's culture), historical particularism* (the theory that each culture is the collective result of a unique historical past), ethnocentrism* (the tendency to judge another culture according to the standards of one's own), cultural history* (roughly, the analysis of cultural traditions by means of the methods of anthropology and history) and material culture* (the artefacts and architecture that provide evidence of a culture).

Boas constructs his arguments well. He draws conclusions following the presentation and explanation of appropriate data according to the inductive anthropological method of his day. More, the text demonstrates how anthropology approaches questions of study in fields such as sociology* (the study of the history and structures of human society), art history,* languages, mythology, Native American* studies, and folklore* studies (the study of traditional stories, songs, crafts, arts, and other forms of cultural knowledge passed on largely through oral communication). Scholars in these and other disciplines, then, will find *Race, Language and Culture* relevant.

Race, Language and Culture also provides an excellent example of scholarship in service of the greater social good. An outspoken critic of scientific racism, Boas understood that theory might employ poor science to achieve racist ends. Boas systematically debunks the claims of racist thinkers, using hard data and robust statistical analysis. He also offers insights into the significance of race, language, and culture in contemporary society.

As Boas saw it, anthropology strives for an understanding of humanity as a whole. He made a positive contribution to anthropology by keeping the discipline focused on shared humanity rather than hierarchical categories. Anthropology teaches us to understand similarity and difference in cultures, without making any single culture more valuable than another. In Boas's view, all cultures are equal in value and no two cultures are the same. Anyone looking for research that argues these points will enjoy reading this book.

SECTION 1
INFLUENCES

MODULE 1
THE AUTHOR AND THE HISTORICAL CONTEXT

KEY POINTS

- As a foundational text in the field of anthropology, *Race, Language and Culture* continues to be relevant today, especially for scholars and students of anthropology and other social sciences.

- Franz Boas grew up in an educated, secular* Jewish, and politically liberal environment in Germany. He pursued higher education in the hard sciences and balanced an appreciation of culture with scientific methodology.

- Boas lived through a time of political upheavals, world conflicts, fascist*—extremely right-wing and nationalistic—governments, and popular movements in which science was employed to racist ends. The historical context of his scholarship emphasizes the significance of his message.

Why Read This Text?

Franz Boas's *Race, Language and Culture* (1940) became a foundational text in the field of anthropology for several reasons.

First, it represents the breadth and depth of Boas's scholarship. In the period in which he worked, the discipline of anthropology was found mainly in the academies of Great Britain and France, where the focus was on what today would be called social anthropology*—a discipline in which culture is considered primarily within social and historical contexts. In these countries, archaeology* and physical anthropology* (the scientific study of the behavior of human beings and our primate and extinct hominid ancestors, also known as

> ❝ My first shock came when one of my ... friends ... declared ... his conviction that one had not the right to doubt what the past had transmitted to us. The shock that this outright abandonment of freedom of thought gave me is one of the unforgettable moments of my life. My whole outlook upon social life is determined by the question: how can we recognize the shackles that tradition has laid upon us? For when we recognize them, we are also able to break them. ❞
>
> Franz Boas, "An Anthropologist's Credo," *Nation*

"biological anthropology") were, and remain, distinct fields of study. American anthropology, however, takes a "four-field approach"* that includes cultural anthropology* (a subfield of anthropology focused on the study of cultural variation among humans groups), linguistics* (the study of the form, meaning, and context of language), physical anthropology,* and archaeology. This approach to anthropology was originated by Franz Boas.[1]

In this text, Boas writes about a wide range of topics. Most anthropologists today specialize in one subfield, but Boas actively studied all of these areas. This both indicates the nature of the field as it then was, being not so rigidly divided into subfields, and reflects Boas's remarkable breadth of knowledge and scholarship.

Second, the text presents Boas's theories of cultural relativism* (the idea that the behavior, beliefs, and actions of an individual are best understood in the context of that person's culture) and historical particularism* (the theory that each culture is the collective result of a unique historical past) as they apply to structuring research and interpreting data. More theoretical chapters integrate his theories into the broader context of the anthropological practice of his day. In other words, the text does not focus just on what anthropology is. It also outlines how to do it.

Third, as we have seen, the text represents a significant step in the creation of a distinctively American style of anthropology. The field of anthropology has not changed much since Boas's day. His work wielded enormous influence on the structure and theoretical scaffolding of American anthropology. Every American anthropologist today somehow follows in his footsteps.

Author's Life

Born in a small town called Minden, in Westphalia, northwestern Germany, Franz Boas was raised by educated, secular Jewish parents. He attended school in his hometown and then continued his studies at a series of universities. Boas studied physics, mathematics and geography,* a particularly favorite subject, before completing his doctorate in physics in 1881 at the University of Kiel* in northern Germany.

After serving a year in the military, Boas joined a German research project in the Arctic. There he studied the relationship between the Inuit*—the indigenous inhabitants then known as "Eskimos"—and the natural environment in which they live. Although he was unsatisfied with the quality of his research, it shifted his interest away from the hard sciences and toward the "desire to understand what determines the behavior of human beings."[2]

After struggling to find employment in the United States, Boas arrived in New York in 1887 to take a job as assistant editor of the prestigious journal *Science.* The position proved to be a tremendous boon to his career. Two years later, he began teaching at Clark University* in Worcester, Massachusetts, which bestowed the first American PhD in anthropology under his tutelage in 1892. He endured a difficult period after the death of his child and then moved to the American Museum of Natural History (AMNH)* in December 1895.

Boas became a full professor at Columbia University* in 1899 and a member of the National Academy of Sciences* the following year. He spent the rest of his career as a prolific author, effective professor, and active research scientist. Franz Boas died at the Columbia Faculty Club in 1942 in the arms of the deeply influential French anthropologist Claude Lévi-Strauss,* then visiting.[3] He was 84 years old.

Author's Background

Boas was born in 1858 and died in 1942. In a lifetime that encompassed both World War I* and the beginning of World War II,* he lived through the worst political upheavals of his day. But he also saw the development of anthropology as a discipline.

Boas was a talented scholar with a passion for his field. Many scholars were developing the methodology of anthropometry,* or measuring the human form, in an attempt to establish a biological, quantitative measurement of race. Scientific racism,* the application of pseudoscience* to support or justify racism and claims of racial superiority, influenced global fascism, political policy, and popular opinion. In the United States and Europe, a popular movement called eugenics* advocated improving the human race through selective breeding. The eugenics movement began in the late nineteenth century and continued for the rest of Boas's life.

Boas's liberal, educated, parents—both secular Jews—were committed to education, social justice, universal suffrage and other progressive democratic reforms. Their son's interest in culture, his commitment to education, and his dedication to social activism all likely reflect his upbringing. As Boas stated, he was raised "in a German home in which the ideals of the Revolution of 1848*—a series of European democratic uprisings—were a living force."[4] He grew up immersed in both German and Jewish culture. Boas's father "retained an emotional affection for the ceremonial of his parental home, without allowing it to influence his intellectual freedom." According to Boas, his parents "had broken through the shackles of dogma."*[5] Boas believed his upbringing shaped his scholarship and his social activism.

NOTES

1   Jerry D. Moore, *Visions of Culture: An Introduction to Anthropological Theories and Theorists* (Lanham, MD: Rowman and Littlefield, 2012), 31–5.

2   Franz Boas, "An Anthropologist's Credo," *Nation* 147 (1938): 201–4. Later revised and reprinted in *I Believe*, ed. Clifton Fadiman (New York: Simon and Shuster, 1939): 19–29.

3   Moore, *Visions of Culture*, 31–5.

4   Boas, "An Anthropologist's Credo," 19.

5   Boas, "An Anthropologist's Credo," 19.

MODULE 2
ACADEMIC CONTEXT

KEY POINTS

- Anthropology is the study of humans, past and present. Scholars in the United States subdivided the discipline into further specialized areas of study.

- At the beginning of the twentieth century, anthropology defined itself in relation to both scientific and humanistic disciplines;* humanistic disciplines focused on the study of human culture. The question of how to understand and explain human variation was a topic of great academic and social interest.

- Franz Boas's work as a scholar, professor, curator and field scientist shaped the direction of twentieth-century American anthropology.

The Work in its Context

Franz Boas published *Race, Language and Culture* in 1940. At the time, anthropology was still a relatively young discipline. In the second half of the eighteenth century, philosophers like Jean-Jacques Rousseau* in France and Johann Gottfried von Herder* in Germany made key contributions to the definition of "culture."[1] Overall, however, anthropology remained most closely allied with the natural sciences,* especially natural history and geology,* as late as the turn of the twentieth century.

Thanks to discoveries in the natural sciences (research into the understanding, description, and prediction of natural phenomena), including the pioneering voyages of the British explorer Captain James Cook* in the eighteenth century, "most of the data of anthropology had been collected by travelers whose primary

> ❝ Anthropology, which was hardly beginning to be a science, ceased at the same time to lose its character of being a single science, but became a method applicable to all the mental sciences, and indispensable to all of them. We are still in the midst of this development. ❞
>
> Franz Boas, "The History of Anthropology"

objective was geographical discovery. To them the relations between man and nature were of prime importance, and their attention was directed less to psychological questions than to those relating to the dependence of the form of culture upon geographical surroundings."[2] We may also see the changing relationship between anthropology and geology, geography* and other natural sciences in Boas's own professional development. He completed a doctorate in physics and undertook a geographical field research project before beginning his pioneering work in anthropology.

Boas conceptualized the scope, methods, and ethics of anthropology very differently from his predecessors—and even his contemporaries across the Atlantic. In the United Kingdom and France, archaeology,* anthropology, and physical anthropology* developed as separate academic disciplines. But because of Boas's wide-ranging research, American anthropology came to include the four subfields of social or cultural anthropology* (the study of cultural variation in human groups), physical anthropology (the study of the behavior of human beings and our ancestors), archaeology (the study of the human past through material remains), and linguistics* (the study of the form and the various meanings and contexts of language). One cannot overstate Boas's influence here. His work shaped the basic assumptions of anthropology in the United States.

Overview of the Field

At the turn of the twentieth century, anthropology sought to explain human variation—in physical appearance, cultural practice, belief, and language. Scholars made advances in geography, biology, and other natural sciences. But an anthropological paradox arose: how to explain the similarities between apparently unrelated cultures. For example, why do we find geometrical and representational* decorative styles around the world, in otherwise different cultures? (Representational art depicts the physical appearance of things.) Before Boas, anthropological scholars took these similarities as proof, in his words, "of the uniform manner in which civilization had developed the world over. The laws according to which this uniform development of culture took place became the new problem which engrossed the attention of anthropologists."[3]

The nineteenth-century British philosopher and anthropologist Herbert Spencer* remains best known today for coining the phrase "survival of the fittest." He and his colleague, the anthropologist Edward Burnett Tylor,* argued that there was " one definite system ... according to which all culture has developed ... from a primitive form to the highest civilizations, which is applicable to the whole of mankind; that, not withstanding many variations ... the general type of evolution is the same everywhere."[4]

In other words, all cultures followed one evolutionary trajectory, progressing from primitive to civilized. It followed, then, that differences in contemporary cultures stemmed from more or less "developed" civilizations. This interpretation was used to justify the classification of human cultures into hierarchies. And Western European scholars saw their own culture as the pinnacle of civilization. Boas challenged many of these assumptions, interpretative methods and conclusions.

Boas began studying anthropology when scholars were just beginning to define it as a discipline. Trying to understand and explain the causes of human diversity, some scholars sought universal rules to apply to all cultures. Franz Boas pioneered an alternative approach. He acknowledged that all people have cultural biases, and worked to objectively understand the development of each culture within the context of its unique cultural history. Boas dedicated his nearly six-decade-long career to this approach.

Academic Influences

Many of Germany's best-known natural scientists influenced Boas. He completed his doctoral research in the field of physics under the supervision of Theobald Fischer,* a German geographer at the University of Kiel.* Fischer himself had been a student of the early nineteenth-century geographer Carl Ritter.* Scholars consider Ritter and the German naturalist and explorer Alexander von Humboldt* the founding figures of modern geography. Boas, then, was not far removed from the influence of pioneering thinkers in the natural sciences.

The philosophy of the eighteenth-century German philosopher Immanuel Kant* also influenced Boas. Kant argued that culture influenced how people thought about moral and universal values. And Boas also engaged with the ideas of the eighteenth-century German philosopher Johann Gottfried von Herder. He was particularly drawn to Herder's idea of individuality, both of cultures[5] and of different people within a culture.[6] Boas built upon this understanding.

Herder had been among the first to argue that language shapes thought.

Another of Boas's influences, the eighteenth-century linguist Wilhelm von Humboldt,* elder brother of Alexander von Humboldt, shared this perspective. The elder Humboldt and Herder had significant influence on the development of the field of linguistics. Nineteenth-century scholars who influenced Boas include the English naturalist Charles Darwin,* considered the founder of modern evolutionary science, the German anthropologist Adolf Bastian,* and the German doctor and anthropologist Rudolf Virchow.*[7] Over the course of his career, Boas absorbed and synthesized an astounding diversity of methods and theories from the natural sciences, philosophy, and psychology.

NOTES

1   Franz Boas, "The History of Anthropology," in *A Franz Boas Reader: The Shaping of American Anthropology, 1883–1911*, ed. George W. Stocking, Jr (Chicago, IL: University of Chicago Press, 1974), 24.

2   Boas, "The History of Anthropology," 25.

3   Boas, "The History of Anthropology," 27.

4   Boas, "The History of Anthropology," 27.

5   Johann Gottfried von Herder, "This Too a Philosophy of History for the Formation of Humanity," in *Philosophical Writings of Johann Gottfried Von Herder*, trans. and ed. Michael N. Forster (Cambridge: Cambridge University Press, 2002).

6   Johann Gottfried von Herder, "On Thomas Abbt's Writings," in *Philosophical Writings of Johann Gottfried Von Herder*; Johann Gottfried von Herder, "On the Cognition and Sensation of the Human Soul," in *Philosophical Writings of Johann Gottfried Von Herder*.

7   Franz Boas, "Rudolf Virchow's Anthropological Work," *Science* 16 (1902): 441–45.

MODULE 3
THE PROBLEM

KEY POINTS

- At the turn of the twentieth century, anthropology focused primarily on the nature, cause, and meaning of human variation. These concerns engaged scholars in the study of archaeological ruins, human physiology, language, and cultural phenomena.

- Scholars eager to apply the theory of Darwinian evolution*— the theory described by the English naturalist Charles Darwin* to explain the development of biological species according to environmental adaptation—began to classify human societies into developmental stages, following a single evolutionary trajectory.

- Franz Boas rejected the idea that all societies followed this single developmental trajectory. Instead, he argued that each society resulted from its own unique cultural history.* He also rejected the hierarchical classification*—roughly, ranking—of cultures according to evolutionary schemes.

Core Question

In *Race, Language and Culture*, Franz Boas addresses a central question of anthropology: what causes differences and similarities between human groups? The topic of natural variation was popular in the natural sciences* of the late nineteenth and early twentieth centuries. Many scientists and scholars of the time focused on taxonomy* (the branch of science concerned with the identification, description, and classification of living organisms), especially in classifying the natural world.

When Charles Darwin published his groundbreaking work *On the Origin of Species** in 1859, he put forth the idea that populations evolve

> ❝ If we grasp the meaning of foreign cultures … in this manner, we shall also be able to see how many of our lines of behavior that we believe to be founded deep in human nature are actually expressions of our culture and subject to modification with changing culture … It is our task to discover among all the varieties of human behavior those that are common to all humanity. By a study of the universality and variety of culture, anthropology may help us to shape the future course of mankind. ❞
>
> Franz Boas, "The Aims of Anthropological Research"

through a process of natural selection. We call this theory Darwinian evolution. Soon, scholars in many fields began attempting to apply the theory of evolution to their own disciplines. Anthropologists were interested in how evolutionary theory might apply to the question of human variation. And that was the state of anthropology before Boas: anthropologists used taxonomy and Darwinian evolution to classify and rank human societies.

Race played a role in this classification as well. Anthropologists engaged in debate on the nature and meaning of race, and how to classify cultures where different races predominated. Many scholars attempted to create scientific or biological definitions to explain racial variations. From our modern perspective, we can see that many (if not most) of these theories used science and pseudoscience*—beliefs and practices incorrectly presented as being based on scientific methods—to achieve racist goals. But the question of race was not just intellectual. It was also one of ethics. Methods of quantifying human variation included measuring skulls and facial features. Scientists applied these methods almost exclusively to communities of color, immigrants Native Americans,* people of mixed race, religious minorities such as Jews, and descendants of enslaved African Americans.

The nature of hereditary traits occupied society as a whole and a movement called eugenics* became popular in the United States. Eugenics sought to maximize "good" traits in the population and minimize undesirable traits. Perhaps not surprisingly, the traits identified as "good" often mirrored the traits of the dominant culture. As a secular* Jewish immigrant—decidedly not a member of the dominant culture—Boas was personally impacted by the anti-Semitic* (hostile to Jewish people and culture) and anti-immigrant attitudes so commonplace in eugenic thought. As a scientist, he was also distinctly qualified to use anthropological data to invalidate scientific racism.* While dismantling the arguments of scientific racism, Boas proposed an alternative vision of what anthropology could and should be as a discipline.

The Participants

Before Boas, cultural or social evolution* (the evolution of human social structures over time) was the dominant theory in anthropology. In particular, the nineteenth-century anthropologists Edward Tylor* and Lewis H. Morgan* advocated for evolutionary frameworks for understanding human cultural diversity.[1] Both were towering figures in the field in Britain (Tylor) and the United States (Morgan), so their opinions carried a great deal of weight. They believed that societies progressed through fixed stages, with European societies representing more advanced states. In their view, non-European societies reflected the "earlier" and "more primitive" forms of societal organization. Archaeology* revealed either the remains of failed cultures or earlier developmental stages of surviving cultures.

Anthropologists in the Tylor–Morgan school looked for universal laws that applied to all cultures.[2] But by the late 1890s, Boas had become an outspoken critic of the evolutionary theories advanced by Tylor and Morgan, among others. Boas took issue with several points but, most importantly, he found that the evolutionary frameworks Tylor and others proposed were untestable and, therefore, unsustainable: "As soon as we admit that the hypothesis of a uniform evolution has to be proved before it can be accepted, the whole structure loses its foundation ... It is clear that if we admit that there may be different ultimate and coexisting types of civilization, the hypothesis of one single general line of development cannot be maintained."[3]

Boas challenged the social evolutionists to support their hypothesis that all civilizations developed according to universal rules. Further, he noted that we can observe multiple kinds of civilizations functioning at the same time in the present moment.

The Contemporary Debate

We may divide the participants in the debate about the nature and cause of human variation into two camps. First, those like Tylor and Morgan who believed that evolutionary schemes could be applied to the development of cultures. Second, Boas—and later, his students—who advocated that we must examine each culture in its own context. Boas also argued that no single culture can be said to be better than another (cultural relativism).* Finally, he made the point that all societies develop as the result of unique culture histories (historical particularism).*

Boas does not explicitly address Tylor's and Morgan's theories in *Race, Language and Culture*. Both had died long before the work's publication, Morgan in 1881 and Tylor in 1917, although Boas, who lived from 1858 to 1942, overlapped with both of them. Morgan was best known in academic circles for his study of kinship structures* (structures and terms defining relationships between related people) among the Native American Iroquois* people (a confederacy of tribes of the northeast United States). He may be seen as an American intellectual predecessor to Boas—although they formed very different conclusions about cultural development.

The English anthropologist Tylor is generally considered the founder of cultural anthropology.* The evolutionary theories of the nineteenth-century British geologist Charles Lyell* particularly influenced him. Tylor postulated that culture develops according to uniform laws, writing: "The condition of culture is a subject apt for the study of laws of human thought and action. On the one hand, the uniformity which so largely pervades civilization may be ascribed … to the uniform action of uniform causes: while on the other hand its various grades may be regarded as stages of development or evolution, each the outcome of previous history, and about to do its proper part in shaping the history of the future."[4]

NOTES

1 Edward Tylor, *Anthropology* (Ann Arbor, MI: University of Michigan Press, 1960), originally published 1881; Edward Tylor, *Researches into the Early History of Mankind and the Development of Civilization* (Chicago, IL: University of Chicago Press, 1964), originally published 1865; Lewis H. Morgan, *Ancient Society; or, Researches in the Line of Human Progress from Savagery through Barbarism to Civilization*, ed. Paul Bohannan (New York: Henry Holt, 1877).

2 Jerry D. Moore, "Founders," in *Visions of Culture: An Introduction to Anthropological Theories and Theorists* (Lanham, MD: Rowman and Littlefield, 2012), 1–2.

3 Franz Boas, "Methods of Cultural Anthropology," in *Race, Language and Culture,* ed. Franz Boas (New York: Macmillan, 1940), 281–2.

4 Edward Tylor, *Primitive Culture* (New York: Harper and Row, 1958), 1, originally published 1920.

MODULE 4
THE AUTHOR'S CONTRIBUTION

KEY POINTS

- Franz Boas argued from a theoretical position that would later become known as cultural relativism:* since people always look first through the lens of their own culture, we cannot objectively define one culture as superior to another.

- Boas presented alternatives to the established theories of social evolution* (explanations of the evolution of human societies). He advocated a broader approach to anthropological questions. This approach still characterizes the modern approach to anthropology, especially in the United States.

- Boas worked with the methods of his day. But he often reached conclusions that contradicted the most popular theories of his time. For example, even though he used anthropometric* data (specific measurements of different human "types"), he used it to argue against scientific racism.*

Author's Aims

In *Race, Language and Culture*, Franz Boas aimed to explain the importance of viewing culture in context, rather than according to hierarchical evolutionary schemes: "The dynamics of life have always been of greater interest to me than the description of conditions, although I recognize that the latter must form the indispensable material on which to base our conclusions. My endeavors have largely been directed by this point of view. In the following pages I have collected such of my writing as, I hope, will prove the validity of my point of view."[1]

> ❝ It is necessary to base the investigation of the mental life of man upon a study of the history of cultural forms and of the interrelations between individual mental life and culture. This is the subject-matter of cultural anthropology.* It is safe to say that the results of the extensive materials amassed during the last fifty years do not justify the assumption of any close relation between biological types and form of culture. ❞
>
> Franz Boas, "The Aims of Anthropological Research"

The essays he included in the text are "not intended to show a chronological development. The plan is rather to throw light on the problems treated. General discussions are followed by reports on special investigations on the results of which general viewpoints are based."[2]

A self-edited volume of previous publications, the work sheds light on Boas's anthropological perspectives concerning the nature of race, language, and culture. As he was more interested in the "dynamics of life" than in the "description of conditions," he did not intend to propose new ways to classify human populations or cultures. Boas defines the aims, scope, and methodology of the discipline of anthropology while presenting his response to important publications and theories of the day.

Approach

Boas's approach in this text has several notable features. First, his selection of publications is almost overwhelmingly diverse. The application of cultural relativism methodology to the study of race, language, and culture unifies the text. Boas did not expect the reader to take his argument at face value. So he gathers a huge amount of data and research to demonstrate that culture is the single greatest explanation for human diversity. This is particularly true for his arguments about race. Boas uses ample statistics to support his argument that races cannot be defined according to biological traits. And he collects his statistics using the commonly accepted anthropometric methods. But Boas arrived at radically different conclusions from those of previous researchers, arguing that culture, not biology, was key to understanding human diversity. In this, he challenged both academic and popular thinkers of the day.

Boas chose to assemble this text from previous publications, rather than write a single great work synthesizing his theories. So the reader must do the work to assimilate the readings and make meaningful connections between chapters. In publishing this collection with minimal reworking, Boas also stands by the validity of his earlier scholarship. This reveals something of the consistency of his theoretical perspective throughout his career.

Contribution in Context

Boas applied the science of his day to anthropological problems. In particular, he was interested in using Darwinian evolution* to explore anthropological questions. Scholars such as the nineteenth-century British anthropologists Edward Tylor,* Herbert Spencer* and Lewis H. Morgan* had previously attempted to apply Charles Darwin's* theories to human societies. They advanced theories of social evolution in which all cultures progressed through the same developmental stages. But in doing so they completely neglected the aspects of adaptation and natural selection that play such an important role in Darwinian theory. This left them virtually no way to explain or to model cultural change. Boas disagreed with the assumption that all cultures necessarily progress through fixed developmental stages. He argued that all societies result from unique historical processes.

As had Darwin, Boas uses a great deal of empirical data to support his arguments. In this way, he is able to demonstrate that in some cases cultural evolutionists* had based their claims either on misinterpreted data or on data that flatly contradicted their conclusions. Today we view some of the scientific methods of the period, especially anthropometry,* as inherently flawed. But anthropology habitually makes use of the best science of the time. Eventually it became clear that Boas's theoretical approach was his most significant contribution to the discipline. Some elements of society had a vested interest in defining race as a biological fact. They also wanted to demonstrate fixed trajectories of social evolution, and to classify human cultures hierarchically. Anthropology became swept up in this movement. By dissenting, Boas helped the discipline to regain its objectivity.

Race, Language and Culture contains essays that document moments of unique scholarship in the development of the field of American anthropology. Boas was both an excellent anthropologist and a great synthesizer. He was able to take the work of others and put it together, while drawing novel insights from the combination. His background in the hard sciences of physics and mathematics may have given him the ability to create methodological approaches to theoretical problems. No one in the field would replicate either his unique way of synthesizing the science of the day or his perspectives on how to approach culture. The theories found in this text would become the foundation for what is now sometimes referred to as "Boasian" anthropology.*

NOTES

. Franz Boas, preface to *Race, Language and Culture,* ed. Franz Boas (New York: Macmillan, 1940), v.

* Boas, preface, v.

SECTION 2
IDEAS

MODULE 5
MAIN IDEAS

KEY POINTS

- Key themes in *Race, Language and Culture* include historical particularism* (the theory that each culture is the collective result of a unique historical past) and cultural relativism* (the idea that the behavior, beliefs, and actions of an individual are best understood in the context of that person's culture).

- In *Race, Language and Culture*, Franz Boas defines the nature, scope, and theory of anthropology, with a focus on understanding the complexity of individual phenomena rather than the creation of general laws.

- Boas intends to convince his reader by using ample evidence that supports his point of view. In this self-edited volume, he presents 62 of his most influential publications selected from a 50-year period.

Key Themes

In *Race, Language and Culture,* Franz Boas presents American anthropology as a historical science, sharing the interpretive goals of history but generating data through scientific methods. The goal of anthropology was broad; "our objective," he writes, is "to understand the steps by which man has come to be what he is, biologically, psychologically and culturally."[1] Since anthropology was concerned with how humans had come to be what they were, its practitioners must understand the history of humanity: "… our material must necessarily be historical … in the widest sense of the term. It must include the history of the development of the bodily form of man, his physiological functions, mind and culture. We need a knowledge of

> 66 In short, the material of anthropology is such that it needs must be a historical science, one of the sciences the interest of which centers in the attempt to understand the individual phenomena rather than in the establishment of general laws which, on account of the complexity of the material, will be necessarily vague and, we might almost say, so self-evident that they are of little help to a real understanding. 99
>
> Franz Boas, "The Aims of Anthropological Research"

the chronological succession of forms and an insight into the conditions under which changes occur."[2]

Boas felt this information was essential to the advancement of the discipline and that without it "progress seems impossible." After defining the goal of anthropology and the importance of collecting cultural historical data, he turns to "the fundamental question [of] how such data [could] be obtained."[3]

Boas relied on two ideas in defining anthropology as a historical science. The first is historical particularism—the idea that each culture is the product of particular historical processes rather than the result of progression through fixed evolutionary stages. The historical particularist presumes all cultures to be of equal value, since each has a unique cultural history.* This perspective is especially clear in the chapters of the work that present ethnographic* research. Before Boas, anthropologists had applied evolutionary theories to classify cultures according to level of "development," usually comparing them to Western Europe as a standard. Historical particularism presented an alternative model, in which cultures, like individual people with unique life histories, result from unique (particular) historical processes.

The second key theme that runs through the text is cultural relativism, a method for understanding the behaviors and beliefs of an individual through the lens of his or her culture. Boas realized that all people—even anthropologists—become influenced by their culture. Ultimately, when we look at foreign cultures we do so through the lens of our own. This idea has become known as cultural relativism. Boas supported this idea with a variety of research that demonstrates the application of the theory. Taken together, these two ideas form the central support for his argument.

Exploring the Ideas

Boas saw historical particularism as paramount: "[Our] very first most immediate object is the study of the history of mankind; not that of civilized nations, but that of the whole of mankind, from its earliest traces found in the deposits of the ice age, up to modern times. We must follow the gradual development of the manifestations of culture."[4] For him, understanding the history of a culture was vital to understanding its present.

This viewpoint stood in stark contrast to contemporary theories that attempted to apply universal laws to cultural development. Scholars supported these theories by arguing that all societies followed the same evolutionary trajectory. Boas did not think anthropology could uncover valid cultural laws that cultures shared universally. Furthermore, he argued that classifying cultures would never adequately explain the variations among them: "Cultural phenomena are of such complexity that it seems to me doubtful whether valid cultural laws can be found. The causal conditions of cultural happenings lie always in the interaction between individual and society, and no classificatory study of societies will solve this problem."[5] Once again, Boas rejects the general in favor of the particular. He emphasizes nuanced interactions between individual and society rather than gross categorizations.

After Boas's death in 1942, scholars coined the term "cultural relativism," attempting to synthesize a unifying theme in his

37

scholarship. Boas had articulated the core of the idea: "civilization is not something absolute … but … is relative, and … our ideas and conceptions are true only so far as our civilization goes."[6] Ultimately, we perceive other cultures through the lens of our own. But to truly understand the beliefs, practices, and behaviors of an individual, we must consider that person within the context of his or her own culture.

Language and Expression

The tone of *Race, Language and Culture* reflects the nature of the discipline of anthropology in 1940. In chapters discussing anthropometry* (measurements taken from different racial "types"), statistics and, more generally, quantitative methods in anthropology (the analysis of numerical data), Boas adopts a scientific tone. Many chapters also integrate statistical analyses of anthropological data. In these chapters, the reader may clearly perceive Boas's background in science.

In the chapters that address questions of what scholars today would call cultural anthropology,* the tone of the text becomes more descriptive. But Boas also includes jargon for cultural phenomena such as kinship systems* (the cultural patterns that provide structure and terminology for identifying relationships between related individuals). Although his writing remains clear throughout, *Race, Language and Culture* is not an easy text. The diversity of topics, the breadth of specialized knowledge it contains, and the clear but somewhat stately nature of Boas's writing sometimes make for a slow read. In addition to well-structured theories, Boas also presents epistemological* questions—questions regarding the nature of knowledge itself—in the discipline. Students may require multiple readings to grasp the full implications of his theories.

The 62 chapters of *Race, Language and Culture* present publications ranging from 1887 to 1937. Boas does not present these works in

chronological order. Rather, he organizes them into three sections—
"Race," "Language," and "Culture." A final "Miscellaneous" section
presents the earliest of his publications, touching on methods for
teaching anthropology, the goals of ethnology* (the study of the
characteristics of various cultures and the relationships between them)
and the study of geography.* Boas includes the latter because "they
indicate the general attitude underlying [his] later work."[7] The
thematic organization of the chapters facilitates theoretical and topical
comparisons throughout. The reader may also take a chronological
approach to the book. Though this would make the work more
difficult to navigate—and run counter to the author's intent—it
would clearly demonstrate the development of Boas's thinking over
time.

NOTES

1   Franz Boas, "The Aims of Anthropological Research," in *Race, Language and Culture,* ed. Franz Boas (New York: Macmillan, 1940), 244.

2   Boas, "The Aims of Anthropological Research," 244.

3   Boas, "The Aims of Anthropological Research," 244.

4   Franz Boas, "The Aims of Ethnology," in *Race, Language and Culture,* ed. Franz Boas (New York: Macmillan, 1940), 628.

5   Boas, "The Aims of Anthropological Research," 257.

6   Franz Boas, "Museums of Ethnology and Their Classification," *Science* 9 (1887): 589.

7   Franz Boas, preface to *Race, Language and Culture,* ed. Franz Boas (New York: Macmillan, 1940), vi.

MODULE 6
SECONDARY IDEAS

KEY POINTS

- Franz Boas presented an alternative perspective on race and worked to separate social and cultural concepts of race from the reality that humans come in many physical varieties. Modern anthropologists now understand "races" as socially constructed groups, not biological categories.

- Boas used anthropological data to invalidate the theories of scientific racism.* And he stressed the notion that fieldwork*—especially cultural immersion, in the course of which the researcher should literally immerse him- or herself in the culture being studied—should be a standard part of anthropological practice.

- His theories also had a profound cultural impact and played a significant role in the development of the early American Civil Rights movement* of the United States in the 1950s and 1960s—the struggle of African American people for equal social and political rights.

Other Ideas

In *Race, Language and Culture*, Franz Boas advances several secondary ideas that made lasting contributions to the field of anthropology. The most significant of these concerns the nature and meaning of race.

Boas dealt with this subject extensively in the text through publications that repudiate scientific racism, pseudoscience* (analysis attempting to pass for science), and the social problem of racism in the United States. In his critique, Boas correctly identified the racism of towering scholars like the eighteenth-century French scholar Georges Cuvier,* known as the father of paleontology (the study of the ancient

> **❝** There is no reason to believe that one race is by nature so much more intelligent, endowed with great will power, or emotionally more stable than another. Nor is there any good reason to believe that the differences between races are so great that the descendants of mixed marriages would be inferior to their parents. **❞**
>
> Franz Boas, "Race and Progress"

past conducted through material evidence such as fossils and artefacts). Cuvier used "science" to justify racist statements such as: "The Negro race ... is marked by black complexion, crisped or woolly hair, compressed cranium and a flat nose. The projection of the lower parts of the face and thick lips, evidently approximate it to the monkey tribe: the hordes of which it consists have always remained in the most complete state of barbarism."[1] Boas debunked such pseudoscience as a poor cover for discrimination and highlighted the reality of racism in society.

Other secondary ideas pertain to anthropological methods, more specifically the nature and role of fieldwork (research conducted outside of the walls of the study) and ethnography* (an anthropological approach in which the beliefs and customs of individuals or cultures are studied and described) within the discipline. Fieldwork has now become a standard practice for anthropology students. But Boas was the first to highlight the importance of extended immersions in other cultures. His early research experience studying the culture of the indigenous Arctic people known as Inuit* (then known as "Eskimos") on Canada's Baffin Island,* undoubtedly informed this perspective: 'A year of life spent ... among Eskimos had a profound influence upon the development of my views, not immediately, but because it ed me away from my former interests and toward the desire to understand what determines the behavior of human beings."[2]

Boas uses his secondary ideas throughout the text to support anthropological interpretations that stress his primary themes of cultural relativism* and historical particularism.* Boas applies these secondary themes to a variety of anthropological studies. In this way, we can best understand the secondary ideas as both a support and an extension of the primary themes of the text.

Exploring the Ideas

Boas fought racist pseudoscience with its own weapons. He used statistical analyses of anthropometric* data to demonstrate that race could not be defined using biological or physical differences. His analyses demonstrated that physical variation is greater between individuals within the same race than between races. Boas measured the heads of immigrant parents and their American-born children and found significant differences. This allowed him to argue that physical form was not a fixed genetic trait but was influenced by the environment. Scientific racists had long viewed the skull as one of the least changeable body parts, which, they believed, made it best suited for defining race. But if the skulls of members of the same race could differ, it threw into question the measurements used for all other racial classifications as well.[3]

Boas lays out an explicit critique of societal racism.* While dismantling the biological definition of race, he also draws attention to societal racism in the United States:"While the biological reasons that are adduced may not be relevant, a stratification of society in social groups that are racial in character will always lead to racial discrimination. As in all other sharp social groupings the individual is not judged as an individual but a member of his class."[4] In other words, racism dehumanizes* individuals—that is, it excludes them from the category of"human"—by treating them as interchangeable members of a general group.

Boas also devotes significant space to discussing the methods of ethnology* (the study of the characteristics of various cultures and the relationships between them) and the goal of anthropological research. In evaluating the limitations of comparative anthropology, he argues that scientists must base all cultural interpretations on the history of each culture, not on broad, general comparisons.[5] These chapters define the scope and nature of anthropological research, highlighting the importance of fieldwork and methodology. They also reinforce the primary ideas of historical particularism and cultural relativism.

Boas argues that cultures do not exhibit any uniform evolution. Instead "each cultural group has its own unique history," dependent both on historical processes unique to that culture and influence from foreign cultures.[6] As a result, "it would be quite impossible to understand, on the basis of a single evolutionary scheme, what happened to any particular people."[7] For Boas, general laws could never adequately explain individual occurrences. Instead, he insists that anthropologists must consider each culture in the context of its unique historical development, not evaluate it against an abstract standard of development.

Overlooked

Boas spoke and published passionately against racism, and *Race, Language and Culture* includes essays that invalidated racism and the scientific definition of race as objectively as possible. But while his contributions to the field have been both wide ranging and long lasting, and his theories are familiar to anthropologists and other social scientists, academic and popular sources frequently overlook his commitment to social and racial justice.

Race, Language and Culture is not a polemic. The text makes only indirect reference to Boas's social and political engagement. But Boas does include several clear and strongly worded statements against racism, scientific racism, and racist policies in the United

43

States. In an address he gave as the president of the American Association for the Advancement of Science in 1931, Boas dismantled race as a biological category. He concluded by challenging his colleagues to address the social reality of racism: "As long as we insist on a stratification in racial layers, we shall pay the penalty in the form of interracial struggle."[8]

While Boas increasingly rejected race as a biological fact, he also drew attention to the social reality of racism and racist policy in the United States at the time. The waves of racial prejudice against African Americans disturbed him greatly. Boas's rejection of race as a biological category laid the foundation for other social scientists to counterattack pseudoscientific race theories. Boas influenced, and worked closely with, scholars and activists in the developing Civil Rights movement, demonstrating the early cooperative relationship between Jewish and African American activists. Boas perceived the link between anti-black, anti-immigrant, and anti-Semitic* prejudices in the United States and understood that undermining any single one of these prejudices undermined them all.[9]

NOTES

1   H. M'Murtrie, trans., *The Animal Kingdom, Arranged in Conformity with Its Organization, by the Baron Cuvier* (New York: Carvill, 1832), 50. Originally published: Georges Cuvier, *Tableau élémentaire de l'histoire naturelle des animaux* (Paris: Baudouin, 1798).

2   Franz Boas, "An Anthropologist's Credo," *The Nation* 147 (1938): 201–4. Later revised and reprinted in *I Believe*, ed. Clifton Fadiman (New York: Simon and Shuster, 1939), 19–29.

3   See, for example: Franz Boas, "Report on Anthropometric Investigation of the Population of the United States," in *Race, Language and Culture*, ed. Franz Boas (New York: Macmillan, 1940), 18–27; Franz Boas, "Changes in Bodily Form of Descendants of Immigrants," in *Race, Language and Culture*, 60–75.

4   Franz Boas, "Race and Progress," in *Race, Language and Culture*, 16–17.

5   Franz Boas, "The Limitations of the Comparative Method of Anthropology,"
    in *Race, Language, and Culture*, 280.

6   Franz Boas, "The Methods of Ethnology," in *Race, Language and Culture*, 286.

7   Boas, "The Methods of Ethnology," 286.

8   Boas, "Race and Progress," 17.

9   Marshall Hyatt, *Franz Boas, Social Activist: The Dynamics of Ethnicity* (New
    York: Greenwood Press, 1990), 84.

MODULE 7
ACHIEVEMENT

KEY POINTS

- Franz Boas altered the course of American anthropology, directing it toward considerations of history and cultural relativism.* He also steered the discipline away from the evolutionary thinking that characterized his predecessors and contemporaries in the European academies.

- In *Race, Language and Culture*, Boas assembled a wide range of scholarship to support his claims. The depth, breadth, and sheer volume of his research provide thorough and convincing evidence.

- The most important limitation on the text was Boas's decision not to edit the publications and produce a more cohesive text. Doing so would have made his argument even clearer and might have made the work more accessible to people outside the discipline.

Assessing the Argument

In *Race, Language and Culture*, Franz Boas outlines the goals and methods of the practice of anthropology. His publications focusing on theory provide an underlying structure that unifies the text. And by publishing the results of his research projects, he demonstrates the relationship between theory and practice. Boas supplies a great deal of information—ethnography* (the study of a people's beliefs and customs), anthropometry* (the study of physical differences between peoples conducted through measurement), reflection, statistical analysis, and linguistic* analysis. This makes it easy for readers to evaluate the robustness of his research.

> ❝ Boas' accomplishments as a teacher, administrator, researcher, founder and president of societies, editor, lecturer and traveller are exhausting to behold. To anyone who has ever worried about publishing or perishing, the fact that all this activity was accompanied by a torrent of books and articles is well nigh terrifying. ❞
>
> Marvin Harris, *The Rise of Anthropological Theory: A History of Theories of Culture*

Boas believed that we could only base cultural interpretation on detailed comparative studies: "When we have cleared up the history of a single culture and understand the effects of environment and the psychological conditions that are reflected in it we have made a step forward, as we can then investigate … how … the same causes or other causes were at work in the development of other cultures … This method is much safer than the comparative method, as it is usually practiced, because instead of a hypothesis of the mode of development actual history forms the basis of our deductions." [1]

Boas found his method was more reliable because he based it on history rather than on a hypothetical model of progress. He buttressed his arguments—and demonstrated the effectiveness of his approach—with a substantial amount of comparative scholarship.

Over his career, Boas established a theoretical and methodological orientation that set American anthropology apart from anthropology as it was practiced in Europe. Boas particularly wanted to establish an American program to train "observers," as he called his anthropology students: "For this reason we have taken up at Columbia* a number of special lines which seem to be most important for carrying on fieldwork, and I here lay particular stress upon a training in linguistics, a general ethnological* training, and knowledge of certain field methods of physical anthropology." *[2]

Race, Language and Culture highlights a historical moment in the development of American anthropology. This vital work did a considerable amount for the entire discipline. Boas did not experience much resistance to the publication of this text, publishing it late in his life when he was already an established scholar. Consequently, the work was well received.

Achievement in Context

Boas's reputation grew over the course of his career. He struggled initially to find an academic post. But his appointment as professor at Columbia University in 1899 and his promotion to curator of anthropology at the American Museum of Natural History (AMNH)* in 1901 gave him both economic and academic freedom. This enabled Boas to write and research prolifically. Boas was elected to the National Academy of Sciences (NAS)* in 1900 and helped to establish the American Anthropological Association (AAA).* He reinvigorated publications such as the journal *American Anthropologist*. In 1917, frustrated by the lack of publication opportunities for papers on linguistic studies, he founded the *International Journal of American Linguistics*.

During his career, Boas published six books and more than 700 articles.[3] Obviously he chose to reprint only a fraction of these in *Race, Language and Culture*. But by 1940, when *Race, Language and Culture* was published, Boas had "played a pivotal role in moving anthropology into academia, in establishing associations and journals, and by creating essential networks of institutional support from the public, policymakers, and other scientists."[4]

Boas did not heavily edit the selections in *Race, Language and Culture*. Perhaps this was a decision influenced by scholarship, but it may have also seemed expedient due to his advancing age. Boas died just two years after the publication of the book. Had he spent more time editing, reworking, or integrating the various chapters, he might not have finished. Another consideration in favor of expedited publication may have been the book's strong anti-racist message. With the outbreak of World War II* in 1939, racist science was spreading across Europe with deadly consequences for Jews and other ethnic, political, sexual, and religious minorities. Boas was strongly committed to social activism throughout his life. It remains difficult, if not impossible, to separate his potential ethical reasons for this publication from academic ones.[5]

Limitations

A primary limitation of *Race, Language and Culture* is the specific nature of the subject matter. The book requires the reader to absorb and manage a challenging amount of specialized knowledge and jargon. Chapters presenting statistical analyses or details of kinship structures*—the ways that people define how they are related to other people—can be difficult to navigate. While the thematic organization of each chapter makes the text easier to do so, the chapters focus on widely varying topics, and Boas leaves it up to the reader to integrate the material into a coherent whole. This may make the text difficult to assimilate; the lay reader may need to consult references for definitions of anthropological terms, statistical methods, and details on the natural sciences.*

Another limitation is that the text leaves out a great deal of Boas's research: "Although *Race, Language, and Culture* ... covered the major aspects of his substantive anthropological work, the focus defined by its title excluded aspects of his career that were perhaps as important and frequently as time-consuming as his actual work," namely "the propagation of anthropology and its application to various issues of general public concern."[6] Boas was an extremely productive scholar. Those interested in pursuing these publications will find in edited volumes of his writings[7] and papers[8] a wealth of additional context and insight into his work.

Boas, an early and outspoken critic of Nazi* Germany, knew about the growing popularity of eugenics.* If he had structured this text differently, contextualized it more directly with the issues of the day, and written in a more generally accessible style, the text might have made a larger impact on American culture as a whole.

NOTES

1   Franz Boas, "Methods of Cultural Anthropology," in *Race, Language and Culture*, ed. Franz Boas (New York: Macmillan, 1940), 279.

2   Franz Boas, "The Boas Plan for American Anthropology," in *A Franz Boas Reader: The Shaping of American Anthropology, 1883–1911*, ed. George W. Stocking, Jr (Chicago, IL: University of Chicago Press, 1974), 287. The content of this chapter is a letter from Franz Boas to Zelia Nutall written in 1901.

3   H. Andrews, "Bibliography of Franz Boas," in *Franz Boas: 1858–1942*, ed. R. Linton (New York: American Anthropological Association).

4   Jerry D. Moore, *Visions of Culture: An Introduction to Anthropological Theories and Theorists* (Lanham, MD: Rowman and Littlefield, 2012), 30.

5   Herbert S. Lewis, "The Passion of Franz Boas," *American Anthropologist* 103, no. 2 (2001), 447–67.

6   George W. Stocking, Jr, preface to *A Franz Boas Reader: The Shaping of American Anthropology, 1883–1911*, ed. George W. Stocking, Jr (Chicago, IL: University of Chicago Press, 1974), vi.

7   George W. Stocking, Jr, ed., *A Franz Boas Reader: The Shaping of American Anthropology, 1883–1911* (Chicago, IL: University of Chicago Press, 1974).

8   Regna Darnell, Michelle Hamilton, Robert L. A. Hancock, and Joshua Smith, eds., *Franz Boas as Public Intellectual—Theory, Ethnography, Activism*, vol. 1 of *The Franz Boas Papers* (Lincoln, NE: University of Nebraska Press, 2015).

MODULE 8
PLACE IN THE AUTHOR'S WORK

KEY POINTS

- Franz Boas produced a great deal of pioneering scholarship over the course of a long and prolific career. He consistently sought to explain cultural processes and to interpret anthropological data through the perspectives of cultural relativism,* historical particularism* and scientific rigor.

- *Race, Language and Culture* brings together Boas's most influential publications. It serves as an excellent introduction to his work and can be used to contextualize his many other publications.

- By the time Boas published Race, Language and Culture, he had already become a well-respected authority in his field. This work cemented Boas's reputation as a pioneer who altered the course of development of American anthropology.

Positioning

Franz Boas published *Race, Language and Culture* in 1940, only two years before he died. The text collects five decades' worth of his most influential publications in the field of anthropology. Boas himself made the selections and edited the volume. He did not intend the text to be a history of his scholarship: "the material presented here is not intended to show a chronological development. The plan is rather to throw light on the problems treated."[1] For the most part, he published the selections without updating them: "On the whole I have left the statements as they first appeared. Only in the discussion of the problems of the stability of races and of growth which extend over many years, has scattered material been combined."[2]

> ❝ This is no ephemeral book; it will long be read, and even belated notice of it is justified. Here the most important papers written by the greatest of American anthropologists, are assembled and arranged in order by Boas himself. It has been characteristic of his work that he has produced no comprehensive syntheses ... This book well represents the nature of his mind; his many-sided interests in the nature of man and culture; his concentration on segregated bodies of controlled fact; his recognition of the complexity of factors entering into social phenomena; and his refusal to be distracted by rhetorical or literary effects. ❞
>
> Robert Redfield, review of *Race, Language and Culture* by Franz Boas

By compiling additional data, Boas strengthened his statistical analyses. Although he acknowledged that scholars still had research to do, he believed his theoretical contributions had value: "It is natural that the earlier papers do not include data available at the present time. I have not made any changes by introducing new material because it seemed to me that the fundamental theoretical treatment of problems is still valid. In a few cases footnotes in regard to new investigations or criticism of the subject matter have been added."[3]

The content of *Race, Language and Culture* reflects Boas's lifelong commitment to anthropological research. A prolific scholar, he wrote six books and more than seven hundred articles. *Race, Language and Culture* contains what Boas considered to be the best and most influential of these publications; those that would "prove the validity of [his] point of view."[4]

Integration

The publications Boas selected for *Race, Language and Culture* show the cohesive nature of his theory and practice over the course of his long career. The chapters function together effectively, despite the fact that Boas edited the text only minimally. This can only be possible because of the underlying unification in Boas's theoretical orientation. Writing about geography* in 1887, Boas stated: "the life of man as far as it depends on the country he lives in—is the true domain of geography."[5] Even at this early stage in his career, we can see that Boas considered the relationship between the general and the specific. He also paid attention to potential causes of variation between groups.

After Boas's death in 1942, scholars coined the term "cultural relativism" to summarize his approach to culture. Many of the selections in *Race, Language and Culture* pertain to cultural relativism, as they demonstrate how Boas consistently attempted to interpret cultural data through the lens of the culture it related to. The term "cultural relativism" also proves useful in providing a structure for integrating the substantial amount of Boas's work that he left out of this text. From beginning to end, Boas's body of work shows that, although he refined and deepened his thinking, he never changed his theoretical orientation.

To contextualize *Race, Language and Culture* within Boas's other work, we must look at the work chronologically. In publishing this text near the end of his life, he did not intend to provide a chronological overview of the development of his thought. Still, the publications he selected cover 50 years of scholarship, so modern scholars interested in the history of anthropology may use them as touchstones.

Significance

Race, Language and Culture remains one of Boas's best-known works, and a foundational text in the study of American anthropology and anthropology of the early twentieth century. Any student of anthropology at undergraduate and graduate levels will want to be familiar with it. By the time Boas published this work, he had already become a towering figure in anthropology—scholar, curator, and professor. This early review could be speaking of the text's continued relevance today: "Dr. Franz Boas has set the pace for American anthropology throughout his long career. His prolific writings have provided stimulus and stability, qualities indispensable to the youthful science struggling toward maturity. Boas' papers … remain sources of frequent and profitable reference. His formulations of problems and suggestions for research continue to bear fruit years after first appearance. His theoretical analyses stand firmly after years of testing."[6]

The selections collected in *Race, Language and Culture* remain some of the most impactful publications Boas produced. Each of these articles enhanced his stature in the field. Reading the chapters in *Race, Language and Culture* in roughly chronological order, one can see Boas becoming ever more certain of his theories and more direct in dismantling scientific racism.*

Many in the generation of scholars whom Boas trained went on to become leading figures in the field of American anthropology in their own right. As his students made positive impacts in the field of anthropology, Boas's reputation continued to spread. The noted American anthropologists he trained included Alfred Kroeber,* Ruth Benedict,* Margaret Mead,* Edward Sapir,* and the novelist and anthropologist Zora Neale Hurston.*

NOTES

1   Franz Boas, preface to *Race, Language and Culture*, ed. Franz Boas (New York: Macmillan, 1940), v.

2   Boas, preface, v–vi.

3   Boas, preface, v–vi.

4   Boas, preface, v.

5   Franz Boas, "The Study of Geography," in *Race, Language and Culture*, ed. Franz Boas (New York: Macmillan, 1940), 640.

6   Verne F. Ray, review of *Race, Language and Culture* by Franz Boas, *Pacific Northwest Quarterly* 31, no. 3 (July 1940): 365–6.

SECTION 3
IMPACT

MODULE 9
THE FIRST RESPONSES

KEY POINTS

- The most important criticisms of Franz Boas's work came from scholars who believed cultural relativism* and historical particularism* were unscientific and overly historical. These scholars advocated science-based models of cultural development.

- After Boas's death in 1942, his students responded to criticisms. They argued for the continued importance and applicability of cultural relativism.

- Boas's method of cultural relativism became increasingly popular during the 1940s. This reflected changes within the discipline of anthropology as well as broad social concern about racism in American society during and after World War II.*

Criticism

Most critics published their responses to Franz Boas's *Race, Language and Culture* shortly after publication of the text. The responses reflected the deep division between Boasian anthropologists* (anthropologists who followed his theoretical framework) and the cultural evolutionists,* who continued to search for universal cultural rules by describing and explaining changes in human society according to the principles of biological evolution. Most reviews of the text were overwhelmingly positive.[1] Many undergraduate and graduate programs began teaching Boasian anthropology as the cutting edge of thought in the discipline.

The main critics of Boas's work came from a younger generation of anthropologists, following in the footsteps of nineteenth-century

66 The result, then, is an excellent 'compilation' of papers heretofore available only in scattered files of professional publications. While there is little that is new to professional students of anthropology, a positive service has been rendered in collecting and arranging these writings, thus making them much more accessible than previously. 99

Rex D. Hopper, review of *Race, Language and Culture* by Franz Boas

cultural evolutionists Edward Burnett Tylor* and Lewis H. Morgan.* Like Tylor and Morgan, these modern critics argued that anthropology could be modeled on the natural laws of physics. They believed the search for these universal laws was of primary importance.[2]

The American anthropologist Leslie White,* who had trained in Boasian anthropology,[3] led the charge. He attacked Boas—often aggressively—in a series of publications.[4] White, along with others such as the Brooklyn-born anthropologist Marvin Harris,* argued that Boas was a historicist,* not a scientist—that he gave primary significance to understanding context, history, geographical place, and culture rather than empirical, rational or scientific approaches.[5] They further criticized Boas for focusing on the unique histories of individual cultures rather than searching for general cultural laws. Had he been alive, Boas would have seen these criticisms as contemporary, updated versions of the cultural evolutionary theories of Tylor, Morgan, and their followers. White, Harris, and other Boas critics remained eager to discover the laws of cultural evolution in much the same way as their intellectual predecessors.[6] While attacking Boas, White was also attempting to revive the reputation of Lewis H. Morgan. He intended to restore the validity of cultural evolutionism.[7]

But other scholars recognized that Boas had pounded the final nail in the coffin of cultural evolutionism. The Australian scholar C. W. M. Hart,* a social anthropologist and sociologist known for his classic works of ethnography,* evaluated the impact that Boas had on the course of anthropological theory:"The work of Dr. Boas and his school has destroyed completely the social evolutionary schemes of Morgan and Tylor."[8] *Race, Language and Culture* contains many of the publications that were instrumental in accomplishing this feat.

Responses

Unfortunately, Boas died before many of these criticisms were published. So he had no opportunity to respond directly. In most cases, his students—many of them outstanding scholars in their own right—took up the task of addressing the critics and defending his theory of cultural relativism. The remarks of Boas's student Alfred Kroeber* reflect an acknowledgement of the relationship between theory and practice in Boasian anthropology. Kroeber also insists on the value of cultural relativism. He acknowledges that it remains problematic to make moral decisions based on moral relativism.* But then he challenges the evolutionists for applying their evolutionary theory so dogmatically.[9] For Kroeber, cultural relativism was not just anthropological theory. It also represented a "common sense" way of understanding cultural diversity. He bristled at the idea that culture could have no more than one evolutionary path. In his view, Boas's hostile critics were intolerant.

The anthropologist Ruth Benedict,* another student of Boas, affirmed the importance of cultural relativism. She continued to emphasize that holding Western civilization as a standard of development reflected ethnocentrism*—the tendency to judge another culture according to the standards of one's own culture—not evolutionary fact. Benedict contrasted anthropology with the natural sciences:"In all the less controversial fields ... the necessary method of study is to group the relevant material and take note of all possible variant forms and conditions. In this way we have learned all that we know of the laws of astronomy, or of the habits of the social insect."[10] She contrasted this with "the major social sciences, [which] have substituted the study of one local variation, that of Western civilization" as a standard of development.[11] Like Boas before her, Benedict remained more interested in studying the variety within and between cultures than in searching for broad, generalizing rules.

Conflict and Consensus

Scholars writing overviews of the history of anthropological theory continue to give Boas a place of prominence. While Boas's impact on the discipline of anthropology is now undeniable, no single consensus has been reached about the relationship between cultural relativism and scientific objectivity.

Leslie White continued to criticize Boas well into the 1960s. Today he is mostly known for his staunch opposition to Boas's theories, rather than for the outstanding or enduring quality of his own research. White's theories remain difficult. He uses idiosyncratic jargon that has, for the most part, become outdated. Boas's theories have had more longevity than White's, providing the foundation for several generations of scholars to make significant contributions to the discipline. Today, we remember Boas not only for his scholarship but because he is "a figure that we in the social sciences find congenial in today's intellectual milieu: egalitarian, individualistic, antifoundational, and politically engaged."[12]

Over the years, Boas's reputation and scholarship have been problematized, analyzed, and contextualized. But his contributions remain striking. Evaluating their importance, Lewis Morgan states: "If Boas' contribution to the understanding of the evolution of culture and social life is less striking than Darwin's contribution to the understanding of biological evolution, perhaps it is because biological evolution is so much simpler."[13]

Advocates continue to praise Boas not only as an impressive scholar but also as "an outstanding and admirable human being, both in terms of what he attempted and what he achieved, in his values and the way in which he put them into practice."[14]

NOTES

1   Rex D. Hopper, review of *Race, Language and Culture* by Franz Boas, *Southwestern Social Science Quarterly* 21, no. 2 (December 1940). See also: Joseph S. Roucek, review of *Race, Language and Culture* by Franz Boas, *Journal of Negro Education* 9, no. 4 (October 1940): 617–8; Robert Redfield, review of *Race, Language and Culture* by Franz Boas, *Annals of the American Academy of Political and Social Science* 214 (March 1941): 265; Verne F. Ray, review of *Race, Language and Culture* by Franz Boas, *Pacific Northwest Quarterly* 31, no. 3 (July 1940): 365–6.

2   Herbert S. Lewis, "Boas, Darwin, Science, and Anthropology," *Current Anthropology* 42, no. 3 (2001): 381–94.

3   Leslie White, *The Evolution of Culture: The Development of Civilization to the Fall of Rome*. (New York: McGraw-Hill, 1959), ix.

4   Leslie White, "Energy and the Evolution of Culture," *American Anthropologist* 45 (1943): 335–56; Leslie White, "Morgan's Attitude toward Religion and Science," *American Anthropologist* 46 (1944); Leslie White, "Diffusion vs. Evolution: An Anti-evolutionist Fallacy," *American Anthropologist* 47 (1945): 218–30; Leslie White, "The Ethnography and Ethnology of Franz Boas," *Bulletin of Texas Memorial Museum* no. 6 (1963): 1–76; Leslie White, "The Social Organization of Ethnological Theory," *Rice University Studies* 52, no. 4 (1966): 1–66.

5   Marvin Harris, *The Rise of Anthropological Theory: A History of Theories of Culture* (New York: Crowell, 1968), 262.

6   Lewis, "Boas, Darwin, Science, and Anthropology," 382.

7   Jerry D. Moore, "Leslie White: Evolution Emergent," in *Visions of Culture: An Introduction to Anthropological Theories and Theorists* (Lanham, MD: Rowman and Littlefield, 2012): 161–73.

8   C. W. M. Hart, "Social Evolution and Modern Anthropology," in *Essays in Political Economy in Honor of E. J. Urwick*, ed. H. A. Innis (Toronto: University of Toronto Press, 1938), 113.

9   Alfred Kroeber, "An Authoritarian Panacea," *American Anthropologist* 51, no. 2 (1949): 319.

10 Ruth Benedict, *Patterns of Culture* (Boston, MA: Houghton Mifflin, 1934), 3.

11 Benedict, *Patterns of Culture*, 3.

12 Michael E. Harkin, Response to Herbert S. Lewis, "Boas, Darwin, Science, and Anthropology," *Current Anthropology* 42, no. 3 (2001): 395.

13 Lewis, "Boas, Darwin, Science, and Anthropology," 403.

14 Lewis, "Boas, Darwin, Science, and Anthropology," 461.

MODULE 10
THE EVOLVING DEBATE

KEY POINTS

- Franz Boas's theories have made an enduring impact in anthropological research and popular social thought. As a result of his work, the discipline of American anthropology evolved very differently in theory, practice, and organization from its European counterpart.

- Though Boas did not coin the term, "cultural relativism"* emerged as a school of thought in anthropology following his death in 1942. Many Boas-trained students went on to develop new areas of inquiry in the subjects of linguistics,* human sexuality, kinship structures,* and folklore* (traditional stories, songs, crafts, arts and other forms of cultural knowledge, largely passed on through oral communication and physical demonstration).

- The concept of anthropological thought—how to understand and value other cultures—entered into popular culture. Boas's work and that of his students influenced scholarship, governmental policy, and important social movements such as the American Civil Rights movement* of the 1950s and 1960s, in the United States.

Uses and Problems

In the decades following its 1940 publication, the central theories in Franz Boas's *Race, Language and Culture* were built upon, tested, and criticized. The most direct continuation of Boas's theories can be found in the work of his students, many of whom would go on to be the next generation of pioneers in anthropology. Two examples are Edward Sapir* and Ruth Benedict.* Other notable students trained

> **"** Franz Boas came to Atlanta University where I was teaching history in 1906 and said to a graduating class: You need not be ashamed of your African past; and then he recounted the history of the black kingdoms of the Sahara for a thousand years. I was too astonished to speak. All of this I had never heard and I came then and afterwards to realize how the silence and neglect of science can let truth utterly disappear or even be unconsciously distorted. **"**
>
> W. E. B. Du Bois, *Black Folk Then and Now*

by Boas include Alfred Kroeber,* Margaret Mead,* and the novelist Zora Neale Hurston.*

Edward Sapir studied Native American* languages with Boas while working on a master's degree in Germanic linguistics. Sapir would later found the modern field of linguistics. Having been exposed to Native American languages by Boas, Sapir experienced a breadth and diversity of human language unusual for the late nineteenth and early twentieth centuries, which inspired his research in the field of linguistics.

Sapir's contemporary Ruth Benedict began studying with Boas in 1921 at Columbia University,* completing her doctorate two years later. She published her seminal work, *Patterns of Culture*, in 1934, arguing that "a culture, like an individual, is a more or less consistent pattern of thought and action." Benedict continued Boas's consideration of the relationship between culture and the individual. She conceptualized culture as "personality writ large." She found that cultures impress certain personality traits on their members.[1]

Benedict also followed in Boas's footsteps by using anthropology to challenge the racist beliefs of her day, writing a pamphlet presenting the scientific case against racist beliefs, illustrated with cartoons: "The peoples of the earth are one family. We all have just so many teeth, so many molars, just so many little bones and muscles—so we can only have come from one set of ancestors no matter what our color, the shape of our head, the texture of our hair. The races of mankind are what the Bible says they are—brothers. In their bodies is the record of their brotherhood."[2]

Schools of Thought

Boas's students engaged with a wide variety of contemporary scientific and philosophical theory as they built upon his understanding of culture. Specifically, his students integrated the theories of the Austrian physicist and philosopher Ernst Mach,* the French mathematician and philosopher Henri Poincaré,* the American psychologist William James,* and the American psychologist and philosopher John Dewey* to the study of anthropological topics. They also pioneered field methods and research topics that greatly strengthened the methodology of the discipline and expanded the subject of anthropological investigation.

The idea of cultural relativism became more popular after World War II,* when people took it to be a doctrine or an ethical position, rather than a scientific method. However, cultural relativism is a scientific method for trying to understand cultural difference objectively, not a world view—a misunderstanding known as "moral relativism,"* according to which ethics and morality are culturally conditioned and, therefore, there is no objective right or wrong. While it is true that culture influences morality, we might consider moral relativism to be a slippery slope. From this perspective, for example, one could not object to racism, sexism, slavery, or even genocide, which could all be argued to be someone else's perception of what is "right."

Boas's scholarship also made a lasting impact in the thinking of early leaders in the American Civil Rights movement;* as Boas biographer Marshall Hyatt put it: "In combination with the interracialism espoused by the National Association for the Advancement of Colored People (NAACP),* the Communist Party of the United States of America (CPUSA), and organized labor, and with W. E. B. Du Bois'* articulation of the need for black economic self-determination and his concern for the masses, Boas' argument helped bring a multidirectional civil rights movement to national attention. His forceful and repetitive attacks on racial injustice led inevitably to more research, and to the gradual invalidation over time of the racists' claim to scientific legitimacy. Once science had abandoned bigotry, the struggle for equality began to chip away at the legal and political hegemony of Jim Crow* society. Boas' legacy in this regard was significant and enduring."[3]

"Jim Crow" here refers to the laws passed to enforce segregation between black and white people in the southern United States at the end of the nineteenth century, many of which continued to be enforced until the 1960s.

In Current Scholarship

Today, scholars consider *Race, Language and Culture* a classic work in American anthropology and continue to engage both with it and with Boas's other publications. The academic response to Boas's critics also continues. In both cases, much of this engagement centers on the theories Boas put forward. This re-contextualization—the application of Boas's ideas to new contexts—reinvigorates Boas's research by producing more nuanced readings of his texts.

More nuanced readings of Boas's texts have also helped scholars round out our understanding of his social activism and personal life. Marshall Hyatt, analyzing Boas's role as a social activist, sets it in the context of Boas's Jewish roots and his personal experiences with anti-Semitism.* Boas remained strongly committed to fighting for the rights of African Americans. Hyatt writes: "He came to the defense of blacks in large measure because he had undergone similar discrimination. ... When he challenged pseudoscientific theory alleging black inferiority, he was reacting to his personal experience. Jews had progressed in all areas of American life, yet anti-Semitism remained alive.... Boas had experienced this firsthand in his dealings with the ... scientific community, which sought to exclude him. By focusing on blacks, he could lay siege to the underpinnings of all forms of racist thought while maintaining scientific objectivity.... If he could abolish racism ..., if he could convince the public that no race was pure and that each made valuable contributions to civilization, perhaps both Jim Crow and anti-Semitism would fall."[4]

Boas does not mention this personal experience in *Race, Language and Culture.* Fuller contextualization helps the reader extract more meaning from the text.

NOTES

1   Margaret Mead, *An Anthropologist at Work: Writings of Ruth Benedict* (New York: Greenwood Press, 1977).

2   Ruth Benedict and Gene Weltfish, *The Races of Mankind*, Public Affairs Pamphlet no. 85 (New York: Public Affairs Committee, Inc. 1943).

3   Marshall Hyatt, *Franz Boas, Social Activist: The Dynamics of Ethnicity* (New York: Greenwood Press, 1990), xi.

4   Hyatt, *Franz Boas, Social Activist*, 97–8.

MODULE 11
IMPACT AND INFLUENCE TODAY

KEY POINTS

- *Race, Language and Culture* stands as a classic text in the field of anthropology.

- The work still challenges readers to consider the nature of fundamental anthropological concepts—race, cultural and linguistic variation, human diversity, individual and culture—while also considering the social and ethical responsibilities of anthropology.

- Current responses to the theoretical and ethical concerns raised by Franz Boas's scholarship fall into two major schools of thought. One school continues to search for universal, scientific laws and the other continues its focus on the historical and individual.

Position

Today, Franz Boas's *Race, Language and Culture* stands as a classic text in the field of anthropology. It is widely recognized as having altered the development of the discipline. Boas's work helped to establish a distinctly American anthropology.

The text is most useful in understanding the historiography*—the study of historical writings, or of the aims and methods of historians—of anthropology. Its key theories and studies shifted the focus of anthropology away from the evolutionary schemes of the nineteenth-century cultural anthropologists* Edward Tylor* and Lewis H. Morgan* and toward a more historical understanding of the discipline. Boas's work laid the foundation for subsequent generations of scholars. Many of Boas's students have continued applying cultural relativism* to a wide range of topics including the nature of kinship,* sexuality,

> ❝ There may be a trajectory leading some anthropologists closer to the scientific philosophy of Franz Boas ... I argue that Boas shows us a way to navigate between the naïve certainties of scientism and positivism on one shore and the nihilistic rejection of science ... on the other. ❞
> Herbert S. Lewis, "Boas, Darwin, Science, and Anthropology"

social patterning* (the theory that cultures are more or less consistent patterns of action and thought), and folklore.*

Through the critical responses to Boas's text, a new school of scientifically oriented anthropology has begun to distinguish itself. These scholars, including critics such as the anthropologists Leslie White* and Marvin Harris,* argued that anthropologists should still search for scientific rules that guide cultural development. They modeled these rules on the hard sciences and hoped they would be universal. In White's words: "Cultural anthropology is that branch of natural science* which deals with matter-and-motion, i.e. energy, phenomena in cultural form, as biology deals with them in cellular, and physics in atomic, form."[1] For White, Harris, and others, the same laws that governed the natural sciences should also govern human culture. They see the difference between anthropology and the natural sciences as one of subject, not approach. Just as physicists study atoms and biologists cells, so anthropologists study the science of culture.

The soft divide between the humanistic and scientific concerns of anthropology continues today. Anthropology remains focused on both the individual and historical as well as the universal and scientific. For example, scholars juxtapose increased attention to underrepresented narratives against discoveries in human genetics

The continued influence of methodological and theoretical trends in the social sciences and the discoveries of science still energize the field today.

Interaction

Current scholars engage with the scholarship of Boas in two main ways.

First, better understandings of the broader philosophical trends in the social sciences during Boas's time allow modern scholars to re-contextualize Boas—that is, to apply his theories to new contexts. This includes situating Boas and his scholarship more thoroughly within the development of anthropology as a whole. For example, the anthropologist Herbert S. Lewis* has resituated Boas within the framework of the American philosophy of his day. Lewis argued that Boas's thought "has significant similarities to that of the American pragmatists,* especially William James,* John Dewey,* and George Herbert Mead* … [It] is clear that Boas and his American contemporaries were exposed to the same general intellectual trends at the time"[2] ("pragmatists" here refers to a philosophical movement that sees the value of thought as an instrument for problem solving). Putting Boas in context allows new evaluations of his scholarship that highlight connections between his thought and broader trends in philosophy and the social sciences.

Second, some scholars have criticized Boas for not making the most out of his research to pursue social justice. In challenging racist theories in the academic world and in society more broadly, Boas was in many ways ahead of his time. Unfortunately, he did not clarify the link between his anti-racist engagement and his research as strongly as he could have. If he had done so, the social implications of his tolerant and humanistic views could have had more of an impact; as one scholar has written: "Although his humanist sympathies often led him to offer his findings in the service of social justice, he did not fully develop the critical potential of historical particularism.*"[3]

By identifying shortcomings in Boas's work, these scholars look for ways to bring the best of his theories into the present. This represents the continued refinement of socially conscious and socially responsible anthropology.

The Continuing Debate

In many ways, anthropology in the twenty-first century remains concerned with the same theoretical, methodological, and ethical questions that inspired Boas's research. In 2007, the United States Army launched the Human Terrain System (HTS),* a program through which social scientists, including anthropologists and linguists, would provide cultural knowledge to military commanders and staff in Afghanistan and Iraq.[4]

From the beginning, the use of anthropological knowledge to achieve military or political outcomes was controversial. In 2007, the Executive Board of the American Anthropological Association (AAA)* issued a statement opposing the HTS, which was found to be in violation of profession codes of ethics for endangering both anthropologists and the people they study: "In the context of a war that is widely recognized as a denial of human rights and based on faulty intelligence and undemocratic principles, the Executive Board sees the HTS project as … an unacceptable application of anthropological expertise."[5] The statement concludes that anthropologists can and should serve government policy only through "robustly democratic processes of fact-finding, debate, dialogue, and deliberation [that] serve the humane causes of global peace and social justice."[6]

In this response, one can hear the echo of Boas's commitment to anthropological ethics. In 1919, he wrote a letter to the editor of the influential magazine *The Nation* in which he criticized the government's use of scientists and anthropologists as spies. "[Proof] has come to my hands that at least four men who carry on anthropologica" work, while employed as government agents, introduced themselves to foreign governments as representatives of scientific institutions in the United States … They have not only shaken the belief in the truthfulness of science, but they have also done the greatest possible disservice to scientific inquiry."[7]

NOTES

1   Leslie White, "Energy and the Evolution of Culture," *American Anthropologist* 45, no. 3 (1943): 335.

2   Herbert S. Lewis, "Boas, Darwin, Science, and Anthropology," *Current Anthropology* 42, no. 3 (2001): 384.

3   Janine Hitchens, "Critical Implications of Franz Boas' Theory and Methodology," *Dialectical Anthropology* 19 (1994): 237.

4   Roberto Gonzalez, "Phoenix Reborn? The Rise of the 'Human Terrain System,'" *Anthropology Today* 23, no. 6 (2007): 21.

5   American Anthropological Association, "Statement on HTS," accessed on 08/29/15. http://www.aaanet.org/issues/policy-advocacy/statement-on-HTS. cfm

6   American Anthropological Association, "Statement on HTS."

7   Franz Boas, "Letter to the Editor," *Nation* 109 (1919): 797. Printed under the heading "Scientists as Spies."

MODULE 12
WHERE NEXT?

KEY POINTS

- *Race, Language and Culture* will continue to occupy an important place in the field of anthropology, serving as a foundational text for future scholars and an inspiration for groundbreaking, holistic scholarship.

- As a discipline, anthropology must, by nature, balance concerns between the specific and universal and the humanistic and the scientific. *Race, Language and Culture* exemplifies how Franz Boas achieved this goal.

- *Race, Language and Culture* established the seeds of a new school of thought in anthropology. Cultural relativism* changed the way anthropologists ask questions, conduct research, and engage with social movements and problems.

Potential

Franz Boas' *Race, Language and Culture* will remain an important text in the discipline of anthropology. Future anthropologists will continue to engage with Boas in theory and practice, much in the same way that biologists engage with Charles Darwin* as a founding figure in that field. While much has changed in the discipline of anthropology since Boas's time, the key questions his research raised continue to be relevant.

The text also offers a historical view of the enduring debate about the ethical responsibilities of anthropology. Today, anthropology combines contemporary science with humanistic and historical understanding. This remains particularly true for the uses of ethnographic* knowledge and the academic and social definition of

> **❝** He seemed to personify the very spirit of science, and with his high seriousness—unsurpassed by any investigator I have known in any sphere—he communicated something of that spirit to others. Therein lies his greatness as a teacher. **❞**
>
> Robert Lowie, "Biographical Memoir of Franz Boas"

race. In 1998, in a "Statement on 'Race,'" the American Anthropological Association (AAA)* argued that "analysis of genetics (e.g. DNA) indicates that most physical variation, about 94 percent, lies *within* so-called racial groups. Conventional geographic 'racial' groupings differ from one another only in about 6 percent of their genes. The continued sharing of genetic materials has maintained all of humankind as a single species."[1] Boas reported the same findings, based on anthropometric* measurements, nearly 50 years earlier: "I believe the present state of our knowledge justifies us in saying that, while individuals differ, biological differences between races are small."[2]

Like Boas, the AAA acknowledges that even though no biological basis for race exists, it remains a problematic social construct: "'Race' thus evolved as a world view, a body of prejudgments that distorts our ideas about human differences and group behavior. Racial beliefs constitute myths about the diversity in the human species and about the abilities and behavior of people homogenized into 'racial' categories. The myths ... imped[e] our comprehension of both biological variations and cultural behavior, implying that both are genetically determined. Racial myths bear no relationship to the reality of human capabilities or behavior. Scientists today find that reliance on such folk beliefs about human differences in research has led to countless errors."[3]

In an increasingly interconnected world, the trends of valuing culture, repudiating scientific racism*—the use of scientific findings for racist ends— and insisting on the ethical practice of anthropology remain relevant today.

Future Directions

Scholars continue to engage with the fundamental theoretical and ethical questions posed by Boas. The AAA has issued several statements about anthropological ethics and the relationship between anthropological evidence and problematic social constructions such as race.

Boas also made a lasting contribution by organizing the discipline into the four subfields of anthropology.* Over time, each of these subfields has developed its own body of scholarship and theory. However, the subfields continue to be unified by methods and theories that reflect broader epistemological* trends in the social sciences— that is, trends in the understanding of what is meant by "knowledge" and how knowledge might be acquired. So any scholar conducting anthropological research today practices method and theory that originated in the scholarship of Franz Boas.

Today, the contemporary British archaeologist Ian Hodder* is known for his scholarship in post-processual archaeology* (a movement that emphasizes that the interpretation of archaeological findings depends on the cultural and social assumptions that the archeologist carries with him or her)—both in theoretical form and in practice through his excavations at the Turkish site of Çatalhöyük* in central Anatolia. In his text *Reading the Past*, Hodder establishes an interpretative position based on the application of cultural relativism He argues that every aspect of daily life for an individual in a culture involves frameworks of meaning. These frameworks are not universal They vary by culture. So, to compare ritual practices, crafts, or subsistence strategies of two different cultures, one cannot separate them from their cultural context. All objects, behaviors, and cultural practices are inherently embedded in their cultural matrix.[4] Hodder's work has extended the application of cultural relativism into a new era.

Summary

Race, Language and Culture constitutes a watershed moment in the field of anthropology. Because of the scholarship collected in this text, American anthropology separated itself from European anthropology on theoretical and methodological grounds. Boas's research addressed many of the fundamental questions in the discipline, such as the nature and meaning of human diversity, the nature of process, and the ethical responsibilities of anthropologists, and polarities such as the universal and the specific, the biological and the cultural, and the historical and the scientific. For these reasons, the text has had a wide-ranging and long-lasting impact on the field, inspiring changes in research topics, interpretive strategies, methods, and theories for several subsequent generations of scholars.

The text remains relevant not only because of its fundamental role in the history of the anthropology, but also because it represents a turning point in the ethical consciousness of the field. Boas was among the first to correctly recognize that anthropologists, as part of their own cultural systems, have a social and ethical responsibility in how anthropological research is collected and applied, and in how they represent their results and interpretations to the general public. Since Boas, anthropologists have been challenged to conduct their research and present their findings ethically.

Boas remains a towering figure in the history of anthropology. Responses to his work have tended to be somewhat polarized. His students and supporters argued not only for the integrity of his theories but also for his integrity as a person. Subsequent scholars have highlighted his scholarship, social activism, commitment to social justice, and strong anti-racist sentiments.

NOTES

1   American Anthropological Association. "Statement on Race," http://www.
     aaanet.org/stmts/racepp.htm. Accessed October 9, 2015.

2   Franz Boas, "Race and Progress," in *Race, Language and Culture*, ed. Franz
     Boas (New York: Macmillan, 1940), 13.

3   American Anthropological Association. "Statement on Race," http://www.
     aaanet.org/stmts/racepp.htm

4   Ian Hodder, *Reading the Past: Current Approaches to Interpretation in
     Archaeology* (Cambridge: Cambridge University Press, 1991).

GLOSSARY

GLOSSARY OF TERMS

Allied forces: the countries united in opposition to the Axis powers of Nazi Germany and its supporters during World War II (1939–45).

American Anthropological Association (AAA): a professional organization of anthropologists in the United States. Founded in 1902, the organization publishes peer-reviewed journals and also hosts an important annual meeting of anthropologists.

American Civil Rights movement (1954–68): a collection of social movements intended to end racial segregation and discrimination against black Americans by securing legal and constitutional guarantee of civil rights for all citizens.

American Museum of Natural History (AMNH): located in New York City, this is one of the largest museums in the world. Its collections contain over 32 million specimens from the natural sciences and artifacts of human cultures.

Anthropometry: the scientific study of the measurements and proportions of the human body. Some anthropologists used anthropometry to support theories of scientific racism during the first half of the twentieth century.

Anti-Semitism: prejudice toward, hatred of, or discrimination against Jewish people on the basis of their religion, ethnicity, or race.

Archaeology: the study of human prehistory based on the analysis of ancient human settlement and material culture.

Art history: the study of artworks for their historical significance, including developments in style, technique, genre, and other formal qualities.

Baffin Island: the largest island in Canada and the traditional land of the Inuit peoples. Boas had his first field experience on Baffin Island, studying Inuit language and culture.

Boasian anthropology: the influential movement in anthropological theory and practice that originated with Franz Boas.

Çatalhöyük: a large archaeological site in modern-day Anatolia, Turkey, dating to the Neolithic and Chalcolithic periods. Çatalhöyük was a regional center and is known today for extensive settlement, religious shrines, and symbolic art and architecture.

Clark University: a private university and liberal arts college in Worcester, Massachusetts. It is the oldest all-graduate institution in the United States. Boas took a position there in 1888 but resigned in 1892 with many other faculty members due to issues of academic freedom.

Columbia University: a private Ivy League research university in New York City. Franz Boas became a professor there in 1896 and founded the first PhD program in anthropology in America.

Cultural anthropology: a subfield of anthropology, focused on the study of cultural variation among human groups. This term is most common in American anthropology, which views culture as a prime mover in creating social dynamics.

Cultural evolutionism: the attempt to describe and explain changes in human society according to the principles of biological evolution.

Cultural history: an approach that combines anthropology and history to analyze cultural traditions and cultural traditions of history. Narrative accounts of knowledge, customs, and cultural practice remain of particular interest in cultural history.

Cultural relativism: the idea that the behavior, beliefs, and actions of an individual are best understood in the context of that person's culture. It was an axiom of Boas's research.

Darwinian evolution: the theory of evolution as developed by the English naturalist Charles Darwin, stating that all organisms arise and develop through natural selection of small, inheritable variations that increase an individual's ability to reproduce, survive, and compete for resources.

Dehumanization: the process of making another group or individual seem less human and, therefore, not worthy of humane treatment. Dehumanization contributes to genocide, war crimes, human rights violations, and violence.

Dogma: principles or beliefs established by an authority to be incontrovertibly true.

Epistemology: the philosophical study of how humans create and understand knowledge. Epistemology focuses not on what we know, but on how we know it.

Ethnocentrism: judging another culture according to the standards of one's own culture. Boas addressed this tendency with the method of cultural relativism.

Ethnography: an anthropological approach in which the beliefs and customs of individuals or cultures are studied and described.

Ethnology: the study of the characteristics of various cultures and the relationships between them.

Eugenics: the social movement claiming to improve genetic qualities in human populations through selective breeding and sterilization. It is based on the idea that some individuals are superior to others, on the basis of race, religion, intelligence, wealth, or other factors.

Fascism: an authoritarian and nationalistic, conservative, extreme right-wing form of governmental or social organization.

Fieldwork: research conducted in the natural environment rather than in laboratories, classrooms, or offices. Anthropological fieldwork often involves spending extended periods of time in a foreign culture.

Folklore: traditional stories, songs, crafts, arts, and other forms of cultural knowledge that are passed on largely through oral communication and physical demonstration. For example, people learn most folk arts through apprenticeship with a more experienced craftsperson, not through formal art education.

"Four-field approach": the division of the field of anthropology into the subfields of archaeology, linguistics, cultural anthropology, and physical anthropology. Boas established this organization of American anthropology and maintained it throughout his career.

Geography: the scientific study of lands, features, inhabitants, and the earth.

Geology: a natural science focusing on the study of the earth, the rocks of which it is made, and the processes by which they change.

Hierarchical classification: a classification system in which entries are arranged based on a hierarchical structure and ranked one above the other according to established criteria.

Historical particularism: a theory formulated by Franz Boas, which argues that each culture is the collective result of a unique historical past.

Historicism: a school of thought that gives primary significance to understanding context, history, geographical place, and culture rather than empirical, rational, or scientific approaches.

Historiography: the study of historical writings.

Human Terrain System (HTS): a program through which social scientists, including anthropologists and linguists, would provide cultural knowledge to military commanders and staff in Afghanistan and Iraq.

Humanistic disciplines: academic disciplines focused on the study of human culture using a variety of critical, comparative, and historical methods. Examples include English, history, art history, and philosophy.

Inuit: a group of Native American and other indigenous peoples who live in Greenland, Canada, and Alaska. In Boas's day, the Inuit people were referred to as Eskimo.

Iroquois: a historically powerful confederacy of Native American tribes in the northeast United States. The Iroquois Confederacy consisted of the Mohawk, Onondaga, Cayuga, Seneca, Tuscarora, and Oneida nations.

Jim Crow: state and local laws enforcing racial segregation and discrimination in the southern United States.

Kinship structures: the cultural patterns that provide structure and terminology for identifying relationships between related individuals.

Linguistics: the scientific study of the form, meaning, and sociocultural context of language.

Material culture: the physical evidence of a culture, as indicated by the objects and architecture produced by that culture.

Moral relativism: the view that morality and ethics are culturally conditioned and, therefore, subjective; an important topic in the philosophy of ethics.

National Academy of Sciences (NAS): a private, non-profit organization in the United States originally founded by Abraham Lincoln to provide independent and objective advice on issues of science and technology.

National Association for the Advancement of Colored People (NAACP): an American civil rights organization founded in 1909, dedicated to eliminating racial discrimination and hatred while advocating for the equal rights of all people.

Native American: indigenous peoples of the United States.

Natural science: a branch of science focused on understanding, describing, and predicting natural phenomena. This is achieved through the interpretation of empirical evidence.

Nazism: a set of political and social beliefs associated with the Nazi Party of Germany, Nazism is a form of fascism that relies on scientific racism and anti-Semitism to argue for the superiority of the Aryan race.

On the Origin of Species: a seminal work by Charles Darwin, published in 1859. In this book, Darwin established his theory of evolution: a theory that would have tremendous impact on the development of the sciences as we know them today.

Physical anthropology (also known as **biological anthropology**): the scientific study of the behavior of human beings and our primate and extinct hominid ancestors.

Post-processual archaeology: a movement of archaeological theory and practice that emphasizes the subjectivity of archaeological interpretations.

Pragmatism: a philosophical movement that sees the value of thought as an instrument for problem solving. Pragmatism began in the United States in 1870. William James, John Dewey, George Herbert Mead, and others were instrumental in establishing pragmatism as a philosophy.

Pseudoscience: a belief, idea, assumption, or opinion that is presented as valid via a false claim of scientific objectivity. Pseudoscience cannot be tested, proven, or validated by the scientific method.

Representational: depicting the physical appearance of things.

Revolution of 1848: also known as the Spring of Nations, this was a series of democratic political upheavals throughout Europe, especially in France, Germany, Italy, and the Netherlands. Upheavals resulted from dissatisfaction with political leadership, demands for freedom of the press, and difficult living conditions for all but the very wealthy.

Scientific racism: the use of pseudoscientific methods, theories, and hypotheses to support racism, schemes of racial inferiority/superiority, and classifying of people into races based on physical appearance.

Secular: beliefs, activities, and lifestyle not based in religious ritual practice.

Social anthropology: generally refers to the practice of cultural anthropology in the British and French universities. Culture is considered primarily within social and historical contexts, and is a result—not a cause of—variation.

Social evolution: the evolution of human social structures over time. This approach originated in the application of evolutionary theory to anthropological questions.

Social patterning: proposed by Ruth Benedict, a theory that states that cultures, like individuals, are more or less consistent patterns of action and thought. Social patterning reflects the continuation of Boas's analysis of the relationship between individual and culture.

Societal racism: racist attitudes within a society.

Sociology: the scientific study of social behavior, order, disorder, and social change.

Taxonomy: the branch of science concerned with the identification, description, and classification of living organisms.

University of Kiel: founded in 1665, the largest, oldest, and most reputable university in the northern German state of Schleswig-Holstein. Boas completed his doctorate in physics at the University of Kiel in 1881.

World War I: a global war from 1914 to 1918 centered in Europe. The war was fought between the Allies (comprised primarily of Britain, France, and the Russian Empire) and the Central Powers (comprised of Germany, Austria-Hungary, the Ottoman Empire, and Bulgaria).

World War II: a global war that lasted from 1939 to 1945. The vast majority of the world's nations aligned to form the Allies and the Axis powers. Mass civilian deaths, including those of the Holocaust (or *Shoah*), along with combat deaths, took a toll of between 50 and 85 million.

PEOPLE MENTIONED IN THE TEXT

Adolf Bastian (1826–1905) was a German scholar best known for his contributions to the development of anthropology as a discipline and his contribution to the development of ethnography.

Ruth Benedict (1887–1948) was an American anthropologist who completed her PhD at Columbia University (1923) with Boas as advisor. She is best known for her *Patterns of Culture*, which focused on the relationship between art, culture, language, and personality.

Captain James Cook (1728–79) was a British Royal Navy captain who successfully circumnavigated the globe in three separate voyages. Cook made lasting contributions in cartography, as he mapped the coastlines of Australia, the Hawaiian Islands, New Zealand, and the Pacific Northwest.

Georges Cuvier (1769–1832) was a French naturalist and zoologist. Sometimes referred to as the father of paleontology, he contributed greatly to natural sciences in the early nineteenth century. He advanced theories of scientific racism and is known for classifying humans into three races.

Charles Darwin (1809–82) was a preeminent English naturalist and geologist who developed the theories of evolution and natural selection based on his observations of the natural world. He published *On the Origin of Species* in 1859.

John Dewey (1859–1952) was an American philosopher and psychologist. He is associated with the philosophy of pragmatism and, along with William James, is viewed as one of the founders of functional psychology.

William Edward Burghardt or W. E. B. Du Bois (1868–1963) was an American sociologist, historian, and civil rights activist. He was one of the co-founders of the NAACP. Du Bois opposed discrimination and racism and was inspired by Boas's theories.

Theobald Fischer (1846–1910) was a German geographer, best known for his contribution to the field of geography and the study of the Mediterranean.

Marvin Harris (1927–2001) was an American anthropologist. Trained in Boasian anthropology, Harris contributed greatly to the study of material culture.

C. W. M. Hart (1905–76) was an Australian social anthropologist and sociologist. Considered an outstanding ethnographer, he is best known for his study of the Tiwi people in Australia.

Johann Gottfried von Herder (1744–1803) was a German philosopher associated with the German Enlightenment.

Ian Hodder (b. 1948) is a British archaeologist best known for pioneering post-processual archaeological theory. Hodder has trained many students who have become leaders in this area of scholarship. He is the project director at the site of Çatalhöyük in Turkey.

Alexander von Humboldt (1769–1859) was a Prussian geographer, naturalist, and explorer. Together with Carl Ritter, he is considered one of the founders of the modern field of geography. He was the younger brother of Wilhelm von Humboldt.

Wilhelm von Humboldt (1767–1835) was a Prussian philosopher, particularly known for his contributions to the study of linguistics. He was the older brother of Alexander von Humboldt.

Zora Neale Hurston (1891–1960) was an American folklorist, anthropologist, and author. She pursued graduate work in anthropology under Boas's tutelage. She made contributions to the field in the area of folklore and is best known for her novel *Their Eyes Were Watching God* (1937).

William James (1842–1910) was an American psychologist who also trained as a physician. Sometimes called the father of American psychology, James was the first to offer a psychology course in the United States. He is associated with the philosophy of pragmatism and helped found the field of functional psychology.

Immanuel Kant (1724–1804) was a German philosopher and a central figure in the establishment of modern philosophy. He argued that categories in the mind structure experience.

Alfred Kroeber (1876–1960) was an American cultural anthropologist who received his PhD at Columbia University (1901) with Boas as advisor, the first such PhD granted by Columbia University.

Claude Lévi-Strauss (1908–2009) was a French anthropologist, best known for his study of the structures of social relationships, his substantial contributions to the study of kinship, and the introduction of structuralism to the field of anthropology.

Herbert S. Lewis (b. 1934) is professor emeritus of anthropology at the University of Wisconsin-Madison. He is noted for his extensive fieldwork and for his defense of the discipline of anthropology from the criticism of post-colonialist thinkers.

Charles Lyell (1797–1875) was a British lawyer and geologist who advanced and popularized the idea that the earth was still being shaped by geological processes that could be observed in the present. His contributions in the field of geology contributed greatly to the understanding of earthquakes, glaciers, and stratigraphy. In particular, Lyell's study of stratigraphy and geological process established the structure for the analysis of the chronological relationships between archaeological deposits.

Ernst Mach (1838–1916) was an Austrian physicist and philosopher, best known for his contributions to the field of physics. He was a major influence on the philosophy of American pragmatism, as expressed by William James, John Dewey, and others.

George Herbert Mead (1863–1931) was an American sociologist and psychologist who helped found the modern practice of American sociology and psychology. He was a pragmatist and conceptualized thought as a practical tool for solving problems.

Margaret Mead (1901–78) was an American anthropologist who studied with Boas and Ruth Benedict. She is best known for her groundbreaking research into human sexuality and social attitudes toward sex.

Lewis Henry Morgan (1818–81) was a pioneering American anthropologist, best known for his theories of social evolution, his work on kinship and social structure, and his ethnography of the Iroquois people.

Henri Poincaré (1854–1912) was a French mathematician and physicist who also focused on the philosophy of free will. Poincaré evaluated the role of intuition and logic in the process of constructing mathematical proofs.

Carl Ritter (1779–1859) was a German scholar considered one of the founders of the modern field of geography, which he conceptualized as analogous to the study of anatomy. He is best known for his encyclopedic publications and theoretical contributions to the developing field of geography.

Jean-Jacques Rousseau (1712–78) was a French philosopher whose political philosophy influenced Enlightenment thinking in France and across Europe.

Edward Sapir (1884–1939) was an American linguist who studied with Franz Boas. He is considered to be the one of the most important figures in the establishment of the modern field of linguistics.

Herbert Spencer (1820–1903) was an English doctor, philosopher, and anthropologist, who developed evolution as a model for all natural occurrences. The phrase "survival of the fittest," often attributed to Charles Darwin, was coined by Spencer in 1864.

Edward Burnett Tylor (1832–1917) was an English anthropologist who is credited with founding the discipline of cultural anthropology. Tylor sought to apply the theories of Charles Lyell and Charles Darwin to the study of human culture and is best known for theories of the stages of cultural evolution.

Rudolf Virchow (1821–1902) was a German doctor, anthropologist, and politician, known for his advancement of public health.

Leslie White (1900–75) was an American anthropologist, best known for advancing theories of cultural evolutionism. He was staunchly opposed to Boasian anthropology and was one of the most vocal and persistent critics of that school of thought.

WORKS CITED

WORKS CITED

American Anthropological Association. "Statement on HTS." Accessed August 29, 2015. http://www.aaanet.org/issues/policy-advocacy/statement-on-HTS.cfm.

"Statement on Race." Accessed October 9, 2015. http://www.aaanet.org/stmts/racepp.htm

Andrews, H. "Bibliography of Franz Boas." In *Franz Boas: 1858–1942*, edited by R. Linton, 67–109. New York: American Anthropological Association, 1943.

Benedict, Ruth. *Patterns of Culture*. Boston, MA: Houghton Mifflin, 1934.

Benedict, Ruth, and Gene Weltfish. *The Races of Mankind*. Public Affairs Pamphlet no. 85. New York: Public Affairs Committee, 1943.

Boas, Franz. "The Aims of Anthropological Research." In *Race, Language and Culture*, edited by Franz Boas, 243–59. New York: Macmillan, 1940. Originally published in *Science* 76 (1932): 605–13.

"The Aims of Ethnology." In *Race, Language and Culture*, edited by Franz Boas, 626–38. New York: Macmillan, 1940. Originally a lecture given before the Deutscher Gesellig-Wissenschaftlicher Verein von New York, March 8, 1888.

"An Anthropologist's Credo." *Nation* 147 (August 1938): 201–4.

"The Boas Plan for American Anthropology." In *A Franz Boas Reader: The Shaping of American Anthropology, 1883–1911*, edited by George W. Stocking, Jr, 287–8. Chicago, IL: University of Chicago Press, 1974.

"Changes in Bodily Form of Descendants of Immigrants." In *Race, Language and Culture*, edited by Franz Boas, 60–75. New York: Macmillan, 1940. Originally published in *American Anthropologist* 14, no. 3 (1912): 530–62.

"The History of Anthropology." In *A Franz Boas Reader: The Shaping of American Anthropology, 1883–1911*, edited by George W. Stocking, Jr, 23–36. Chicago, IL: University of Chicago Press, 1974. Originally published in *Science* (October 1904): 513–24.

"Letter to the Editor," *Nation* 109 (1919): 797. Printed under the heading "Scientists as Spies."

"The Limitations of the Comparative Method of Anthropology." In *Race, Language and Culture*, edited by Franz Boas, 270–80. New York: Macmillan, 1940. Originally published in *Science* 4 (1896): 901–8.

"The Methods of Ethnology." In *Race, Language and Culture*, edited by Franz Boas, 281–9. New York: Macmillan, 1940. Originally published in *American Anthropologist* 22 (1920): 311–21.

"Museums of Ethnology and Their Classification." *Science* 9 (1887): 578–89.

Preface to *Race, Language and Culture*, edited by Franz Boas, v–vi. New York: Macmillan, 1940.

"Race and Progress." In *Race, Language and Culture*, edited by Franz Boas, 3–17. New York: Macmillan, 1940. Originally published in *Science* 74 (1931): 1–8.

Race, Language and Culture. New York: MacMillan, 1940.

"Report on Anthropometric Investigation of the Population of the United States." In *Race, Language and Culture*, edited by Franz Boas, 28–59. New York: Macmillan, 1940. Originally published in Journal of the *American Statistical Association* 18 (1922): 181–209.

"Rudolf Virchow's Anthropological Work." *Science* 16 (1902): 441–5.

"The Study of Geography." In *Race, Language and Culture*, edited by Franz Boas, 639–47. New York: Macmillan, 1940. Originally published in *Science* 9 (1887): 137–41.

Cuvier, Georges. *Tableau élémentaire de l'histoire naturelle des animaux.* Paris: Baudouin, 1798.

Darnell, Regna, Michelle Hamilton, Robert L. A. Hancock, and Joshua Smith, eds. *Franz Boas as Public Intellectual – Theory, Ethnography, Activism.* Vol. 1 of *The Franz Boas Papers*. Lincoln, NE: University of Nebraska Press, 2015.

Du Bois, W. E. B. *Black Folk Then and Now: An Essay in the History and Sociology of the Negro.* New York: Octagon, 1970.

Fadiman, Clifton, ed. *I Believe: The Personal Philosophies of Certain Eminent Men and Women of Our Time.* New York: Simon and Schuster, 1939.

Gonzalez, Roberto. "Phoenix Reborn? The Rise of the 'Human Terrain System.'" *Anthropology Today* 23, no. 6 (2007): 21–2.

Harkin, Michael E. Response to Herbert S. Lewis, "Boas, Darwin, Science, and Anthropology." *Current Anthropology* 42, no. 3 (2001): 395–6.

Harris, Marvin. *The Rise of Anthropological Theory: A History of Theories of Culture.* New York: Crowell, 1968.

Hart, C. W. M. "Social Evolution and Modern Anthropology." In *Essays in Political Economy in Honor of E. J. Urwick*, edited by H. A. Innis, 99–116. Toronto: University of Toronto Press, 1938.

Herder, Johann Gottfried von. "On the Cognition and Sensation of the Human Soul." In *Philosophical Writings of Johann Gottfried Von Herder*, translated and edited by Michael N. Forster, 187–243. Cambridge: Cambridge University Press 2002.

"On Thomas Abbt's Writings." In *Philosophical Writings of Johann Gottfried Von Herder*, translated and edited by Michael N. Forster, 167–77. Cambridge: Cambridge University Press, 2002.

"This Too a Philosophy of History for the Formation of Humanity." In *Philosophical Writings of Johann Gottfried Von Herder*, translated and edited by Michael N. Forster, 268–71. Cambridge: Cambridge University Press, 2002.

Hitchens, Janine. "Critical Implications of Franz Boas' Theory and Methodology." *Dialectical Anthropology* 19 (1994): 237–53.

Hodder, Ian. *Reading the Past: Current Approaches to Interpretation in Archaeology.* Cambridge: Cambridge University Press, 1991.

Hopper, Rex D. Review of *Race, Language and Culture* by Franz Boas. *Southwestern Social Science Quarterly* 21, no. 2 (December 1940): 278–9.

Hyatt, Marshall. *Franz Boas, Social Activist: The Dynamics of Ethnicity.* New York: Greenwood Press, 1990.

Kroeber, Alfred. "An Authoritarian Panacea." *American Anthropologist* 51, no. 2 (1949): 318–20.

Lewis, Herbert S. "Boas, Darwin, Science, and Anthropology." *Current Anthropology* 42, no. 3 (2001): 381–94.

"The Passion of Franz Boas." *American Anthropologist* 103, no. 2 (2001): 447–67.

Lowie, Robert H. "Biographical Memoir of Franz Boas 1858–1942." National Academy of Sciences 24, Ninth Memoir (1947): 303–22.

Mead, Margaret. *An Anthropologist at Work: Writings of Ruth Benedict.* New York: Greenwood Press, 1977.

M'Murtrie, H., trans. *The Animal Kingdom, Arranged in Conformity with Its Organization, by the Baron Cuvier.* New York: Carvill, 1832.

Moore, Jerry D. *Visions of Culture: An Introduction to Anthropological Theories and Theorists.* Lanham, MD: Rowman and Littlefield, 2012.

Morgan, Lewis H. *Ancient Society; or, Researches in the Line of Human Progress from Savagery through Barbarism to Civilization.* New York: Henry Holt, 1877.

Ray, Verne F. Review of *Race, Language and Culture* by Franz Boas. *Pacific Northwest Quarterly* 31, no. 3 (July 1940): 365–6.

Redfield, Robert. Review of *Race, Language and Culture* by Franz Boas. *Annals of the American Academy of Political and Social Science* 214 (1941): 265.

Roucek, Joseph. Review of *Race, Language and Culture* by Franz Boas. *Journal of Negro Education* 9, no. 4 (October 1940): 617–18.

Stocking, George W., Jr, ed. *A Franz Boas Reader: The Shaping of American Anthropology, 1883–1911.* Chicago, IL: University of Chicago Press, 1974.

Preface to *A Franz Boas Reader: The Shaping of American Anthropology, 1883–1911*, edited by George W. Stocking, Jr. Chicago, IL: University of Chicago Press, 1974.

Tylor, Edward. *Anthropology.* Ann Arbor, MI: University of Michigan Press, 1960. Originally published as *Anthropology: An Introduction to the Study of Man and Civilization.* London: Macmillan, 1881.

Primitive Culture. New York: Harper and Row, 1958. Originally published as *Primitive Culture: Researches into the Development of Mythology, Philosophy, Religion, Language, Art, and Custom.* London: John Murray, 1920.

Researches into the Early History of Mankind and the Development of Civilization, edited by Paul Bohannan. Chicago, IL: University of Chicago Press, 1964.

White, Leslie. "Diffusion vs. Evolution: An Anti-evolutionist Fallacy." *American Anthropologist* 47 (1945): 339–56.

"Energy and the Evolution of Culture." *American Anthropologist* 45 (1943): 335–56.

"The Ethnography and Ethnology of Franz Boas." *Bulletin of Texas Memorial Museum* no. 6 (1963): 1–76.

The Evolution of Culture: The Development of Civilization to the Fall of Rome. New York: McGraw-Hill, 1959.

"Morgan's Attitude toward Religion and Science." *American Anthropologist* 46 (1944): 218–30.

"The Social Organization of Ethnological Theory." *Rice University Studies* 52, no. 4 (1966): 1–66.

THE MACAT LIBRARY
BY DISCIPLINE

AFRICANA STUDIES

Chinua Achebe's *An Image of Africa: Racism in Conrad's Heart of Darkness*
W. E. B. Du Bois's *The Souls of Black Folk*
Zora Neale Huston's *Characteristics of Negro Expression*
Martin Luther King Jr's *Why We Can't Wait*
Toni Morrison's *Playing in the Dark: Whiteness in the American Literary Imagination*

ANTHROPOLOGY

Arjun Appadurai's *Modernity at Large: Cultural Dimensions of Globalisation*
Philippe Ariès's *Centuries of Childhood*
Franz Boas's *Race, Language and Culture*
Kim Chan & Renée Mauborgne's *Blue Ocean Strategy*
Jared Diamond's *Guns, Germs & Steel: the Fate of Human Societies*
Jared Diamond's *Collapse: How Societies Choose to Fail or Survive*
E. E. Evans-Pritchard's *Witchcraft, Oracles and Magic Among the Azande*
James Ferguson's *The Anti-Politics Machine*
Clifford Geertz's *The Interpretation of Cultures*
David Graeber's *Debt: the First 5000 Years*
Karen Ho's *Liquidated: An Ethnography of Wall Street*
Geert Hofstede's *Culture's Consequences: Comparing Values, Behaviors, Institutes and Organizations across Nations*
Claude Lévi-Strauss's *Structural Anthropology*
Jay Macleod's *Ain't No Makin' It: Aspirations and Attainment in a Low-Income Neighborhood*
Saba Mahmood's *The Politics of Piety: The Islamic Revival and the Feminist Subjec*t
Marcel Mauss's *The Gift*

BUSINESS

Jean Lave & Etienne Wenger's *Situated Learning*
Theodore Levitt's *Marketing Myopia*
Burton G. Malkiel's *A Random Walk Down Wall Street*
Douglas McGregor's *The Human Side of Enterprise*
Michael Porter's *Competitive Strategy: Creating and Sustaining Superior Performance*
John Kotter's *Leading Change*
C. K. Prahalad & Gary Hamel's *The Core Competence of the Corporation*

CRIMINOLOGY

Michelle Alexander's *The New Jim Crow: Mass Incarceration in the Age of Colorblindness*
Michael R. Gottfredson & Travis Hirschi's *A General Theory of Crime*
Richard Herrnstein & Charles A. Murray's *The Bell Curve: Intelligence and Class Structure in American Life*
Elizabeth Loftus's *Eyewitness Testimony*
Jay Macleod's *Ain't No Makin' It: Aspirations and Attainment in a Low-Income Neighborhood*
Philip Zimbardo's *The Lucifer Effect*

ECONOMICS

Janet Abu-Lughod's *Before European Hegemony*
Ha-Joon Chang's *Kicking Away the Ladder*
David Brion Davis's *The Problem of Slavery in the Age of Revolution*
Milton Friedman's *The Role of Monetary Policy*
Milton Friedman's *Capitalism and Freedom*
David Graeber's *Debt: the First 5000 Years*
Friedrich Hayek's *The Road to Serfdom*
Karen Ho's *Liquidated: An Ethnography of Wall Street*

John Maynard Keynes's *The General Theory of Employment, Interest and Money*
Charles P. Kindleberger's *Manias, Panics and Crashes*
Robert Lucas's *Why Doesn't Capital Flow from Rich to Poor Countries?*
Burton G. Malkiel's *A Random Walk Down Wall Street*
Thomas Robert Malthus's *An Essay on the Principle of Population*
Karl Marx's *Capital*
Thomas Piketty's *Capital in the Twenty-First Century*
Amartya Sen's *Development as Freedom*
Adam Smith's *The Wealth of Nations*
Nassim Nicholas Taleb's *The Black Swan: The Impact of the Highly Improbable*
Amos Tversky's & Daniel Kahneman's *Judgment under Uncertainty: Heuristics and Biases*
Mahbub Ul Haq's *Reflections on Human Development*
Max Weber's *The Protestant Ethic and the Spirit of Capitalism*

FEMINISM AND GENDER STUDIES

Judith Butler's *Gender Trouble*
Simone De Beauvoir's *The Second Sex*
Michel Foucault's *History of Sexuality*
Betty Friedan's *The Feminine Mystique*
Saba Mahmood's *The Politics of Piety: The Islamic Revival and the Feminist Subject*
Joan Wallach Scott's *Gender and the Politics of History*
Mary Wollstonecraft's *A Vindication of the Rights of Woman*
Virginia Woolf's *A Room of One's Own*

GEOGRAPHY

The Brundtland Report's *Our Common Future*
Rachel Carson's *Silent Spring*
Charles Darwin's *On the Origin of Species*
James Ferguson's *The Anti-Politics Machine*
Jane Jacobs's *The Death and Life of Great American Cities*
James Lovelock's *Gaia: A New Look at Life on Earth*
Amartya Sen's *Development as Freedom*
Mathis Wackernagel & William Rees's *Our Ecological Footprint*

HISTORY

Janet Abu-Lughod's *Before European Hegemony*
Benedict Anderson's *Imagined Communities*
Bernard Bailyn's *The Ideological Origins of the American Revolution*
Hanna Batatu's *The Old Social Classes And The Revolutionary Movements Of Iraq*
Christopher Browning's *Ordinary Men: Reserve Police Batallion 101 and the Final Solution in Poland*
Edmund Burke's *Reflections on the Revolution in France*
William Cronon's *Nature's Metropolis: Chicago And The Great West*
Alfred W. Crosby's *The Columbian Exchange*
Hamid Dabashi's *Iran: A People Interrupted*
David Brion Davis's *The Problem of Slavery in the Age of Revolution*
Nathalie Zemon Davis's *The Return of Martin Guerre*
Jared Diamond's *Guns, Germs & Steel: the Fate of Human Societies*
Frank Dikotter's *Mao's Great Famine*
John W Dower's *War Without Mercy: Race And Power In The Pacific War*
W. E. B. Du Bois's *The Souls of Black Folk*
Richard J. Evans's *In Defence of History*
Lucien Febvre's *The Problem of Unbelief in the 16th Century*
Sheila Fitzpatrick's *Everyday Stalinism*

Eric Foner's *Reconstruction: America's Unfinished Revolution, 1863-1877*
Michel Foucault's *Discipline and Punish*
Michel Foucault's *History of Sexuality*
Francis Fukuyama's *The End of History and the Last Man*
John Lewis Gaddis's *We Now Know: Rethinking Cold War History*
Ernest Gellner's *Nations and Nationalism*
Eugene Genovese's *Roll, Jordan, Roll: The World the Slaves Made*
Carlo Ginzburg's *The Night Battles*
Daniel Goldhagen's *Hitler's Willing Executioners*
Jack Goldstone's *Revolution and Rebellion in the Early Modern World*
Antonio Gramsci's *The Prison Notebooks*
Alexander Hamilton, John Jay & James Madison's *The Federalist Papers*
Christopher Hill's *The World Turned Upside Down*
Carole Hillenbrand's *The Crusades: Islamic Perspectives*
Thomas Hobbes's *Leviathan*
Eric Hobsbawm's *The Age Of Revolution*
John A. Hobson's *Imperialism: A Study*
Albert Hourani's *History of the Arab Peoples*
Samuel P. Huntington's *The Clash of Civilizations and the Remaking of World Order*
C. L. R. James's *The Black Jacobins*
Tony Judt's *Postwar: A History of Europe Since 1945*
Ernst Kantorowicz's *The King's Two Bodies: A Study in Medieval Political Theology*
Paul Kennedy's *The Rise and Fall of the Great Powers*
Ian Kershaw's *The "Hitler Myth": Image and Reality in the Third Reich*
John Maynard Keynes's *The General Theory of Employment, Interest and Money*
Charles P. Kindleberger's *Manias, Panics and Crashes*
Martin Luther King Jr's *Why We Can't Wait*
Henry Kissinger's *World Order: Reflections on the Character of Nations and the Course of History*
Thomas Kuhn's *The Structure of Scientific Revolutions*
Georges Lefebvre's *The Coming of the French Revolution*
John Locke's *Two Treatises of Government*
Niccolò Machiavelli's *The Prince*
Thomas Robert Malthus's *An Essay on the Principle of Population*
Mahmood Mamdani's *Citizen and Subject: Contemporary Africa And The Legacy Of Late Colonialism*
Karl Marx's *Capital*
Stanley Milgram's *Obedience to Authority*
John Stuart Mill's *On Liberty*
Thomas Paine's *Common Sense*
Thomas Paine's *Rights of Man*
Geoffrey Parker's *Global Crisis: War, Climate Change and Catastrophe in the Seventeenth Century*
Jonathan Riley-Smith's *The First Crusade and the Idea of Crusading*
Jean-Jacques Rousseau's *The Social Contract*
Joan Wallach Scott's *Gender and the Politics of History*
Theda Skocpol's *States and Social Revolutions*
Adam Smith's *The Wealth of Nations*
Timothy Snyder's *Bloodlands: Europe Between Hitler and Stalin*
Sun Tzu's *The Art of War*
Keith Thomas's *Religion and the Decline of Magic*
Thucydides's *The History of the Peloponnesian War*
Frederick Jackson Turner's *The Significance of the Frontier in American History*
Odd Arne Westad's *The Global Cold War: Third World Interventions And The Making Of Our Times*

LITERATURE

Chinua Achebe's *An Image of Africa: Racism in Conrad's Heart of Darkness*
Roland Barthes's *Mythologies*
Homi K. Bhabha's *The Location of Culture*
Judith Butler's *Gender Trouble*
Simone De Beauvoir's *The Second Sex*
Ferdinand De Saussure's *Course in General Linguistics*
T. S. Eliot's *The Sacred Wood: Essays on Poetry and Criticism*
Zora Neale Huston's *Characteristics of Negro Expression*
Toni Morrison's *Playing in the Dark: Whiteness in the American Literary Imagination*
Edward Said's *Orientalism*
Gayatri Chakravorty Spivak's *Can the Subaltern Speak?*
Mary Wollstonecraft's *A Vindication of the Rights of Women*
Virginia Woolf's *A Room of One's Own*

PHILOSOPHY

Elizabeth Anscombe's *Modern Moral Philosophy*
Hannah Arendt's *The Human Condition*
Aristotle's *Metaphysics*
Aristotle's *Nicomachean Ethics*
Edmund Gettier's *Is Justified True Belief Knowledge?*
Georg Wilhelm Friedrich Hegel's *Phenomenology of Spirit*
David Hume's *Dialogues Concerning Natural Religion*
David Hume's *The Enquiry for Human Understanding*
Immanuel Kant's *Religion within the Boundaries of Mere Reason*
Immanuel Kant's *Critique of Pure Reason*
Søren Kierkegaard's *The Sickness Unto Death*
Søren Kierkegaard's *Fear and Trembling*
C. S. Lewis's *The Abolition of Man*
Alasdair MacIntyre's *After Virtue*
Marcus Aurelius's *Meditations*
Friedrich Nietzsche's *On the Genealogy of Morality*
Friedrich Nietzsche's *Beyond Good and Evil*
Plato's *Republic*
Plato's *Symposium*
Jean-Jacques Rousseau's *The Social Contract*
Gilbert Ryle's *The Concept of Mind*
Baruch Spinoza's *Ethics*
Sun Tzu's *The Art of War*
Ludwig Wittgenstein's *Philosophical Investigations*

POLITICS

Benedict Anderson's *Imagined Communities*
Aristotle's *Politics*
Bernard Bailyn's *The Ideological Origins of the American Revolution*
Edmund Burke's *Reflections on the Revolution in France*
John C. Calhoun's *A Disquisition on Government*
Ha-Joon Chang's *Kicking Away the Ladder*
Hamid Dabashi's *Iran: A People Interrupted*
Hamid Dabashi's *Theology of Discontent: The Ideological Foundation of the Islamic Revolution
in Iran*
Robert Dahl's *Democracy and its Critics*
Robert Dahl's *Who Governs?*
David Brion Davis's *The Problem of Slavery in the Age of Revolution*

Alexis De Tocqueville's *Democracy in America*
James Ferguson's *The Anti-Politics Machine*
Frank Dikotter's *Mao's Great Famine*
Sheila Fitzpatrick's *Everyday Stalinism*
Eric Foner's *Reconstruction: America's Unfinished Revolution, 1863-1877*
Milton Friedman's *Capitalism and Freedom*
Francis Fukuyama's *The End of History and the Last Man*
John Lewis Gaddis's *We Now Know: Rethinking Cold War History*
Ernest Gellner's *Nations and Nationalism*
David Graeber's *Debt: the First 5000 Years*
Antonio Gramsci's *The Prison Notebooks*
Alexander Hamilton, John Jay & James Madison's *The Federalist Papers*
Friedrich Hayek's *The Road to Serfdom*
Christopher Hill's *The World Turned Upside Down*
Thomas Hobbes's *Leviathan*
John A. Hobson's *Imperialism: A Study*
Samuel P. Huntington's *The Clash of Civilizations and the Remaking of World Order*
Tony Judt's *Postwar: A History of Europe Since 1945*
David C. Kang's *China Rising: Peace, Power and Order in East Asia*
Paul Kennedy's *The Rise and Fall of Great Powers*
Robert Keohane's *After Hegemony*
Martin Luther King Jr.'s *Why We Can't Wait*
Henry Kissinger's *World Order: Reflections on the Character of Nations and the Course of History*
John Locke's *Two Treatises of Government*
Niccolò Machiavelli's *The Prince*
Thomas Robert Malthus's *An Essay on the Principle of Population*
Mahmood Mamdani's *Citizen and Subject: Contemporary Africa And The Legacy Of Late Colonialism*
Karl Marx's *Capital*
John Stuart Mill's *On Liberty*
John Stuart Mill's *Utilitarianism*
Hans Morgenthau's *Politics Among Nations*
Thomas Paine's *Common Sense*
Thomas Paine's *Rights of Man*
Thomas Piketty's *Capital in the Twenty-First Century*
Robert D. Putman's *Bowling Alone*
John Rawls's *Theory of Justice*
Jean-Jacques Rousseau's *The Social Contract*
Theda Skocpol's *States and Social Revolutions*
Adam Smith's *The Wealth of Nations*
Sun Tzu's *The Art of War*
Henry David Thoreau's *Civil Disobedience*
Thucydides's *The History of the Peloponnesian War*
Kenneth Waltz's *Theory of International Politics*
Max Weber's *Politics as a Vocation*
Odd Arne Westad's *The Global Cold War: Third World Interventions And The Making Of Our Times*

POSTCOLONIAL STUDIES

Roland Barthes's *Mythologies*
Frantz Fanon's *Black Skin, White Masks*
Homi K. Bhabha's *The Location of Culture*
Gustavo Gutiérrez's *A Theology of Liberation*
Edward Said's *Orientalism*
Gayatri Chakravorty Spivak's *Can the Subaltern Speak?*

PSYCHOLOGY

Gordon Allport's *The Nature of Prejudice*
Alan Baddeley & Graham Hitch's *Aggression: A Social Learning Analysis*
Albert Bandura's *Aggression: A Social Learning Analysis*
Leon Festinger's *A Theory of Cognitive Dissonance*
Sigmund Freud's *The Interpretation of Dreams*
Betty Friedan's *The Feminine Mystique*
Michael R. Gottfredson & Travis Hirschi's *A General Theory of Crime*
Eric Hoffer's *The True Believer: Thoughts on the Nature of Mass Movements*
William James's *Principles of Psychology*
Elizabeth Loftus's *Eyewitness Testimony*
A. H. Maslow's *A Theory of Human Motivation*
Stanley Milgram's *Obedience to Authority*
Steven Pinker's *The Better Angels of Our Nature*
Oliver Sacks's *The Man Who Mistook His Wife For a Hat*
Richard Thaler & Cass Sunstein's *Nudge: Improving Decisions About Health, Wealth and Happiness*
Amos Tversky's *Judgment under Uncertainty: Heuristics and Biases*
Philip Zimbardo's *The Lucifer Effect*

SCIENCE

Rachel Carson's *Silent Spring*
William Cronon's *Nature's Metropolis: Chicago And The Great West*
Alfred W. Crosby's *The Columbian Exchange*
Charles Darwin's *On the Origin of Species*
Richard Dawkin's *The Selfish Gene*
Thomas Kuhn's *The Structure of Scientific Revolutions*
Geoffrey Parker's *Global Crisis: War, Climate Change and Catastrophe in the Seventeenth Century*
Mathis Wackernagel & William Rees's *Our Ecological Footprint*

SOCIOLOGY

Michelle Alexander's *The New Jim Crow: Mass Incarceration in the Age of Colorblindness*
Gordon Allport's *The Nature of Prejudice*
Albert Bandura's *Aggression: A Social Learning Analysis*
Hanna Batatu's *The Old Social Classes And The Revolutionary Movements Of Iraq*
Ha-Joon Chang's *Kicking Away the Ladder*
W. E. B. Du Bois's *The Souls of Black Folk*
Émile Durkheim's *On Suicide*
Frantz Fanon's *Black Skin, White Masks*
Frantz Fanon's *The Wretched of the Earth*
Eric Foner's *Reconstruction: America's Unfinished Revolution, 1863-1877*
Eugene Genovese's *Roll, Jordan, Roll: The World the Slaves Made*
Jack Goldstone's *Revolution and Rebellion in the Early Modern World*
Antonio Gramsci's *The Prison Notebooks*
Richard Herrnstein & Charles A Murray's *The Bell Curve: Intelligence and Class Structure in American Life*
Eric Hoffer's *The True Believer: Thoughts on the Nature of Mass Movements*
Jane Jacobs's *The Death and Life of Great American Cities*
Robert Lucas's *Why Doesn't Capital Flow from Rich to Poor Countries?*
Jay Macleod's *Ain't No Makin' It: Aspirations and Attainment in a Low Income Neighborhood*
Elaine May's *Homeward Bound: American Families in the Cold War Era*
Douglas McGregor's *The Human Side of Enterprise*
C. Wright Mills's *The Sociological Imagination*

Thomas Piketty's *Capital in the Twenty-First Century*
Robert D. Putman's *Bowling Alone*
David Riesman's *The Lonely Crowd: A Study of the Changing American Character*
Edward Said's *Orientalism*
Joan Wallach Scott's *Gender and the Politics of History*
Theda Skocpol's *States and Social Revolutions*
Max Weber's *The Protestant Ethic and the Spirit of Capitalism*

THEOLOGY

Augustine's *Confessions*
Benedict's *Rule of St Benedict*
Gustavo Gutiérrez's *A Theology of Liberation*
Carole Hillenbrand's *The Crusades: Islamic Perspectives*
David Hume's *Dialogues Concerning Natural Religion*
Immanuel Kant's *Religion within the Boundaries of Mere Reason*
Ernst Kantorowicz's *The King's Two Bodies: A Study in Medieval Political Theology*
Søren Kierkegaard's *The Sickness Unto Death*
C. S. Lewis's *The Abolition of Man*
Saba Mahmood's *The Politics of Piety: The Islamic Revival and the Feminist Subject*
Baruch Spinoza's *Ethics*
Keith Thomas's *Religion and the Decline of Magic*

COMING SOON

Chris Argyris's *The Individual and the Organisation*
Seyla Benhabib's *The Rights of Others*
Walter Benjamin's *The Work Of Art in the Age of Mechanical Reproduction*
John Berger's *Ways of Seeing*
Pierre Bourdieu's *Outline of a Theory of Practice*
Mary Douglas's *Purity and Danger*
Roland Dworkin's *Taking Rights Seriously*
James G. March's *Exploration and Exploitation in Organisational Learning*
Ikujiro Nonaka's *A Dynamic Theory of Organizational Knowledge Creation*
Griselda Pollock's *Vision and Difference*
Amartya Sen's *Inequality Re-Examined*
Susan Sontag's *On Photography*
Yasser Tabbaa's *The Transformation of Islamic Art*
Ludwig von Mises's *Theory of Money and Credit*

Macat Pairs

Analyse historical and modern issues from opposite sides of an argument. Pairs include:

HOW TO RUN AN ECONOMY

John Maynard Keynes's
The General Theory OF Employment, Interest and Money

Classical economics suggests that market economies are self-correcting in times of recession or depression, and tend toward full employment and output. But English economist John Maynard Keynes disagrees.

In his ground-breaking 1936 study *The General Theory*, Keynes argues that traditional economics has misunderstood the causes of unemployment. Employment is not determined by the price of labor; it is directly linked to demand. Keynes believes market economies are by nature unstable, and so require government intervention. Spurred on by the social catastrophe of the Great Depression of the 1930s, he sets out to revolutionize the way the world thinks

Milton Friedman's
The Role of Monetary Policy

Friedman's 1968 paper changed the course of economic theory. In just 17 pages, he demolished existing theory and outlined an effective alternate monetary policy designed to secure 'high employme stable prices and rapid growth.'

Friedman demonstrated that monetary policy plays a vital role in broader economic stability and argued that economists got their monetary policy wrong in the 1950s and 1960s by misunderstanding the relationship between inflation and unemployment. Previous generations of economists had believed that governments could permanently decrease unemployment by permitting inflation—and vice ve Friedman's most original contribution was to show this supposed trade-off is an illusion that only work the short term.

Macat analyses are available from all good bookshops and libraries

Access hundreds of analyses through one, multimedia tool.
Join free for one month **library.macat.com**

Macat Disciplines

Access the greatest ideas and thinkers across entire disciplines, including

THE FUTURE OF DEMOCRACY

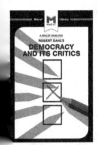

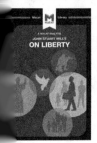

Robert A. Dahl's, *Democracy and Its Critics*
Robert A. Dahl's, *Who Governs?*
Alexis De Toqueville's, *Democracy in America*
Niccolò Machiavelli's, *The Prince*
John Stuart Mill's, *On Liberty*
Robert D. Putnam's, *Bowling Alone*
Jean-Jacques Rousseau's, *The Social Contract*
Henry David Thoreau's, *Civil Disobedience*

Macat Disciplines

Access the greatest ideas and thinkers across entire disciplines, including

TOTALITARIANISM

Sheila Fitzpatrick's, *Everyday Stalinism*
Ian Kershaw's, *The "Hitler Myth"*
Timothy Snyder's, *Bloodlands*

Macat Pairs

Analyse historical and modern issues from opposite sides of an argument. Pairs include:

RACE AND IDENTITY

Zora Neale Hurston's
Characteristics of Negro Expression

Using material collected on anthropological expeditions to the South, Zora Neale Hurston explains how expression in African American culture in the early twentieth century departs from the art of white America. At the time, African American art was often criticized for copying white culture. For Hurston, this criticism misunderstood how art works. European tradition views art as something fixed. But Hurston describes a creative process that is alive, ever-changing, and largely improvisational. She maintains that African American art works through a process called 'mimicry'—where an imitated object or verbal pattern, for example, is reshaped and altered until it becomes something new, novel—and worthy of attention.

Frantz Fanon's
Black Skin, White Masks

Black Skin, White Masks offers a radical analysis of the psychological effects of colonization on the colonized.

Fanon witnessed the effects of colonization first hand both in his birthplace, Martinique, and again later in life when he worked as a psychiatrist in another French colony, Algeria. His text is uncompromising in form and argument. He dissects the dehumanizing effects of colonialism, arguing that it destroys the native sense of identity, forcing people to adapt to an alien set of values—including a core belief that they are inferior. This results in deep psychological trauma.

Fanon's work played a pivotal role in the civil rights movements of the 1960s.

Macat Pairs

Analyse historical and modern issues from opposite sides of an argument. Pairs include:

INTERNATIONAL RELATIONS IN THE 21ˢᵀ CENTURY

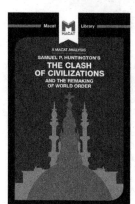

Samuel P. Huntington's
The Clash of Civilisations

In his highly influential 1996 book, Huntington offers a vision of a post-Cold War world in which conflict takes place not between competing ideologies but between cultures. The worst clash, he argues, will be between the Islamic world and the West: the West's arrogance and belief that its culture is a "gift" to the world will come into conflict with Islam's obstinacy and concern that its culture is under attack from a morally decadent "other."

Clash inspired much debate between different political schools of thought. But its greatest impact came in helping define American foreign policy in the wake of the 2001 terrorist attacks in New York and Washington

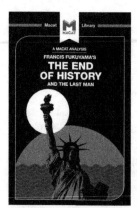

Francis Fukuyama's
The End of History and the Last Man

Published in 1992, *The End of History and the Last Man* argues that capitalist democracy is the final destination for all societies. Fukuyama believed democracy triumphed during the Cold War because it lacks the "fundamental contradictions" inherent in communism and satisfies our yearning for freedom and equality. Democracy therefore marks the endpoint in the evolution of ideology, and so the "end of history." There will still be "events," but no fundamental change in ideology.

Macat analyses are available from all good bookshops and libraries

Access hundreds of analyses through one, multimedia tool.

Join free for one month **library.macat.com**

Macat Disciplines

*Access the greatest ideas and thinkers
across entire disciplines, including*

MAN AND THE ENVIRONMENT

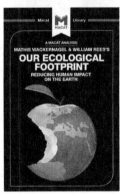

The Brundtland Report's, *Our Common Future*

Rachel Carson's, *Silent Spring*

James Lovelock's, *Gaia: A New Look at Life on Earth*

athis Wackernagel & William Rees's, *Our Ecological Footprint*

cat analyses are available from all good bookshops and libraries.

Access hundreds of analyses through one, multimedia tool.

Join free for one month **library.macat.com**

Printed in the United States
by Baker & Taylor Publisher Services